High Sierra
Climbing

California's Best High Country Climbs

High Sierra Climbing

California's Best High Country Climbs

Chris McNamara

Published by
SuperTopo
2 Bradford Way
Mill Valley, CA 94941
www.supertopo.com

Topos and text by Chris McNamara, Todd Vogel, SP Parker, and Greg Barnes
History by Steve Roper, Andy Selters, and Erik Sloan
Managing Editor and Designer: Sarah Felchlin
Senior Editor and Head of Shipping: Steve McNamara
Copyeditor: DeAnne Musolf Crouch
Publisher: Chris McNamara

Front cover: Dave Miller Startrekkin' (5.10c) on Mt. Russell's remarkable clean
and exposed south face. *Photo by PatitucciPhoto.*
Frontispiece: First light on Cathedral Peak, Tuolumne's most sought after summit.
Photo by PatitucciPhoto.
Back cover: The Whitney Crest: the High Sierra's mini-version of Patagonia.
Photo by PatitucciPhoto.

McNamara, Chris
High Sierra Climbing: California's Best High Country Climbs

ISBN 0-9672391-8-4

Contents

Warning!

Climbing is an inherently dangerous sport in which severe injuries or death may occur. Relying on the information in this book may increase the danger.

When climbing you can only rely on your skill, training, experience, and conditioning. **If you have any doubts as to your ability to safely climb any route in this guide, do not try it.**

This book is neither a professional climbing instructor nor a substitute for one. **It is not an instructional book. Do not use it as one.** It contains information that is nothing more than a compilation of opinions about climbing in the High Sierra. **These opinions are neither facts nor promises.** Treat the information as opinions and nothing more. Do not substitute these opinions for your own common sense and experience.

Assumption of Risk

There may be errors in this book resulting from the mistakes of the authors and/or the people with whom they consulted. The information was gathered from a variety of sources, which may not have been independently verified. Those who provided the information may have made mistakes in their descriptions. The authors may have made mistakes in their conveyance of the information in this book. **The authors cannot, therefore, guarantee the correctness of any of the information contained in this book.** The topographical maps, photo-diagrams, difficulty ratings, protection ratings, approach and/or descent information, suggestions about equipment, and other matters may be incorrect or misleading. Fixed protection may be absent, unreliable, or misplaced. **You must keep in mind that the information in this book may be erroneous, so use your own judgement when choosing, approaching, climbing, or descending from a route described in this book.**

DO NOT USE THIS BOOK UNLESS YOU [AND YOUR ESTATE] PROMISE NEVER TO SUE US IF YOU GET HURT OR KILLED.

Disclaimer of Warranties

THE AUTHORS AND PUBLISHER WARN THAT THIS BOOK CONTAINS ONLY THE AUTHORS' OPINIONS ON THE SUBJECTS DISCUSSED. THEY MAKE NO OTHER WARRANTIES, EXPRESSED OR IMPLIED, OF MERCHANTABILITY, FITNESS FOR PURPOSE, OR OTHERWISE, AND IN ANY EVENT, THEIR LIABILITY FOR BREACH OF ANY WARRANTY OR CONTRACT WITH RESPECT TO THE CONTENT OF THIS BOOK IS LIMITED TO THE PURCHASE PRICE OF THE BOOK. THEY FURTHER LIMIT TO SUCH PURCHASE PRICE THEIR LIABILITY ON ACCOUNT OF ANY KIND OF NEGLIGENT BEHAVIOR WHATSOEVER ON THEIR PART WITH RESPECT TO THE CONTENTS OF THIS BOOK.

Acknowledgements

Huge thanks to: **Dana Benson** for tolerating my sandbagging on the Northeast Ridge of Bear Creek Spire. We later realized the route is not "4th class" and bulky hiking boots are not ideal for soloing exposed 5.5 on your first Sierra climb. **Peter Croft** for tons of beta and leading me up (sans ropes, of course) my first High Sierra 14er. **Sarah Felchlin** who did an awesome job managing, editing, and laying out this guidebook and forgave me when I got way off route on the Fishhook Arête. **Brad Goya** for joining me on many of the climbs and insisting that I was wasting my time by climbing in any alpine setting other than the High Sierra. **Aaron Martin, Joey Papazian,** and **Paul Wignall** for a great Incredible Hulk trip. **Steve Levinson** and two-one-eight for reminding me that as cool as the High Sierra is, the Valley is still where it's at. **Gene Malone** for his thorough editing and feedback. My dad **Steve McNamara** who is not only Senior Editor and Head of Shipping, but has also been a huge inspiration and endless source of good advice. My mom **Kay McNamara** who never wavers in her support. **Morgan McNamara,** bro, who makes sure that the SuperTopo Mill Valley office is always having fun. **Marshall Minobe** for beta and photos on the SuperTopo web site as well as working hard on Eastern Sierra community building and environmental protection (www.easternsierraadvocates.org). **Russell Mitrovich** for beta, posing, and waiting for me on the approaches. **Todd Offenbacher** for way too much fun on many climbing trips to The Hulk, Conness, etc. **SP Parker, Todd Vogel,** and **Sierra Mountain Center** who provided great photos, topos, and beta for Temple Crag and Charlotte Dome. **Steve Roper** for history and introduction text. **Karen Roseme** for lots of beta and route suggestions. **Mick Ryan** and Rockfax guidebooks for editing topos and being a great help in general. **David Safanda** for continued, awesome work on the SuperTopo web site. **Andy Selters** for the great histories. **Erik Sloan** for badass advice, research, and general assistance with this book as well as selfless service to the climbing community in general. **Doug Thompson** for great beta on the Mountaineer's Route and delicious hamburgers at the Whitney Portal Store.

Thank you everyone who sent feedback: Allen L Binette, Tony Brake, Zeanid Breyer, Gary Clark, Cori Constantine, Mary Hollendoner, Joe Lemay, Anthony Longobardo, Kristin Tara McNamara, Bob Odom, Scott Rogers, Thomas Rogers, Florence Scholl, and Cedar Wright.

Lastly, I want to thank two people who are no longer with us. **Galen and Barbara Rowell** were close friends and mentors. Their friendship, encouragement, and unrelenting energy revealed a more passionate and creative world to me. While I miss them, we are all fortunate that they published almost 20 books that captured their love for the mountains. It's hard to open *Mountain Light* or *High and Wild* and not want to experience wild places. In the end, that's why I publish books. Hopefully you, the reader, will drop whatever you are doing, load up the car, and break out for the mountains.

— *Chris McNamara*

ACCESS: It's every climber's concern

The Access Fund, a national, non-profit climbers' organization, works to keep climbing areas open and to conserve the climbing environment. Need help with closures? Land acquisition? Legal or land management issues? Funding for trails and other projects? Starting a local climbers' group? CALL US!

Climbers can help preserve access by being committed to leaving the environment in its natural state. Here are some simple guidelines:

• **ASPIRE TO CLIMB WITHOUT LEAVING A TRACE,** especially in environmentally sensitive areas like caves. Chalk can make a significant impact on dark and porous rock—don't use it around historic rock art. Pick up litter, and leave trees and plants intact.

• **DISPOSE OF HUMAN WASTE PROPERLY.** Use toilets whenever possible. If toilets are not available, dig a "cat hole" at least six inches deep and 200 feet from any water, trails, campsites, or the base of climbs. *Always pack out toilet paper.* On big wall routes, use a "poop tube" and carry waste up and off with you (the old "bag toss" is now illegal in many areas).

• **USE EXISTING TRAILS.** Cutting across switchbacks causes erosion. When walking off-trail, tread lightly, especially in the desert where cryptogamic soils (usually a dark crust) take thousands of years to form and are easily damaged. Be aware that "rim ecologies" (the clifftop) are often highly sensitive to disturbance.

• **BE DISCREET WITH FIXED ANCHORS.** *Bolts are controversial and are not a convenience—don't place them unless they are really necessary.* Camouflage all anchors. Remove unsightly slings from rappel stations (better to use steel chain or welded cold shuts). Bolts sometimes can be used proactively to protect fragile resources—consult with your local land manager.

• **RESPECT THE RULES** and speak up when other climbers don't. Expect restrictions in designated wilderness areas, rock art sites, caves, and in sensitive wildlife areas such as nesting sites for birds of prey. *Power drills are illegal in wilderness areas and all national parks.*

• **PARK AND CAMP IN DESIGNATED AREAS.** Some climbing areas require a permit for overnight camping.

• **MAINTAIN A LOW PROFILE.** Leave the boom box and day-glo clothing at home. The less climbers are seen and heard, the better.

• **RESPECT PRIVATE PROPERTY.** Be courteous to land owners. Don't climb where you're not wanted.

• **JOIN THE ACCESS FUND.** To become a member, make a tax-deductible donation of $25.

THE ACCESS FUND
Keeping climbing areas open and conserving the climbing environment
P.O. Box 17010
Boulder, CO 80308

A deadly bolt more than 20 years old … one of several
thousand on popular climbs throughout the United States.

A new bolt rated to over 5,000 pounds. The ASCA
wants to replace the bad bolt above with one of these.

Bad Bolts Kill

We need YOUR help. The American Safe Climbing Association has helped replace more than
4,500 bolts throughout the country. We estimate that there are more than 20,000 bad bolts
remaining on popular climbs today. Your $50 donation will make at least one route safe . . . and
that one route could be the next one you climb. The ASCA would like to get there before you do.

Does your crag need
re-bolting? Please
contact us.

asca
American Safe Climbing Association

❏ $25 Supporter   ❏ $50 Contributor   ❏ $100 Advocate   ❏ $500 Lifer

Name

Address

E-Mail/Phone

All contributors receive the ASCA newsletter.
Make checks payable to: ASCA, 2 Bradford Way, Mill Valley, CA 94941
or donate online at www.safeclimbing.org

The American Safe Climbing Association is a 501(c)3 organization and contributions are tax-deductible.

Introduction

The view west from the summit of Mt. Russell.

Bordered by a great agricultural area on one side and an inhospitable desert on the other, California's Sierra Nevada is the highest mountain range in the contiguous United States, and some say it is the most beautiful. It has almost everything a climber desires: rugged peaks, glaciers, and splendid, isolated chunks of granite. And these attractions are set in a lovely locale of lake basins, streams, and high meadows. The rock is generally good, the weather during the summer months is excellent, and the access is easy. What more could a climber want? If there is any disadvantage, it lies in the hordes of people who have recently found the range to their liking. The John Muir Trail, which runs the length of the High Sierra, is a crowded corridor in mid-summer, yet the climber who is willing to wander just a few miles from it will find untrammeled lake basins at the base of peaks that see fewer than ten ascents a year.

Long ago the Spaniards saw the range and gave it its present name, which means "snowy range of mountains." In former times the 300-mile-long uplift posed a serious threat to east-west travel, and even now there are no roads across its most rugged portion for 175 miles. The crest of the range, which runs from northwest to southeast, contains scores of peaks above 13,000 feet, and 12 peaks rise above 14,000 feet. Nestled under the western side of the crest are hundreds of lakes, some set in high glacial basins and some surrounded by lush meadows.

The western side of the range slopes gently. It is nearly 50 miles from the Central Valley to the crest, and much of this distance is marked by heavy and varied forests. Scattered amid these forests are groves of "big trees," or sequoias. These enormous trees, endemic to the western slope of the Sierra, are one of the great tourist attractions of the West, and a national park has been named for them.

The summits themselves are often easiest to reach from the west, and almost every Sierra peak has at least one side that presents no problem for the climber. The north and east faces, however, tend to be steeper and have often been sculpted by glaciers.

The eastern escarpment of the High Sierra is a magnificent sight. Along its base runs U.S. 395, and from it the traveler can gaze upward nearly 2 vertical miles to see the range's culmination: Mt. Whitney. Roads that lead into the range begin in vast fields of sagebrush, wind through the pinyon-juniper belt, and finally pass through several varieties of pine. Driving up such a road one can experience a temperature drop of 20 degrees.

Much of the rock in the Sierra is granite of excellent quality; some, in fact, is world-renowned by rockclimbers. The rock in

Mark Leffler on the North Ridge of Bear Creek Spire. (PatitucciPhoto)

the high country is heavily fractured, and although the rock itself may be solid, the disjointed structure makes for many loose blocks. The vast amount of rubble on ledges is proof that the mountains are continually falling to pieces. In addition to igneous rock, a few places such as the Ritter Range, Black Divide, and the Kaweahs are principally metamorphic, and some exceptionally loose rock is found in these areas. The climber must take every precaution on this type of rock.

Glaciers were active in the range for many centuries, and although only a few remnants survive, evidence of them abounds. The Kern River Valley, remarkably straight and U-shaped, is one of the finest examples of glacial action in the High Sierra, but almost every other valley shows prominent signs of the ice sheets that once scoured them.

General Climbing History

Indians were the first climbers of the High Sierra, as has been shown by arrowhead fragments found high on many peaks, including Mt. Whitney. But the Indians left no records, and neither did the Spaniards, early military expeditions, prospectors, or sheepherders who followed. However, it is not likely that many major summits were reached during these early days, for as we all know, there are relatively few reasons to stand atop a mountain.

During the Gold Rush, thousands crossed the Sierra Nevada, but they all carefully avoided the highest and most rugged part of the range. By the time of the Civil War, California had become a populated state, yet little was known about its resources or geography. It was to rectify this deplorable situation that the legislature created the California Geological Survey in 1860. For a few years the Whitney Survey, as it soon became called after its leader, Josiah Whitney, did work in other parts of the state, moving into the Sierra foothills only in the summer of 1863. After spending time in the fabulous, recently discovered Yosemite Valley, the Survey climbed up toward Tuolumne Meadows. There,

William Brewer, field leader of the Survey, Charles Hoffmann, and Whitney climbed a prominent peak, which they named Mt. Hoffmann. This is the first known ascent of a major peak in the High Sierra (Mt. Tom, near Bishop, may have been climbed in 1860). A few days later Brewer and Hoffmann climbed a very high summit that they named Mt. Dana, after the pre-eminent American geologist of the era. They thought the peak was higher than Mt. Shasta, which at that time was considered the highest point in the state. The next day Whitney climbed the peak to see the view; it was his last important Sierra climb, and he soon left the range to direct from afar. From then on Brewer and his associates dominated the Survey's mountaineering.

Without question, 1864 is the key year in the history of early Sierra climbing and exploration. That year the Survey was composed of Brewer, Hoffmann, Clarence King, James Gardiner, and the group's packer, Richard Cotter. Leaving Oakland in late May, they rode their mounts eastward. It was the driest summer in many years, and the party suffered in the oppressive heat. Mummified carcasses of cattle lay everywhere and dusty whirlwinds darted across the grasslands. It must have been a welcome relief to reach the mountains, which they did in early July in the vicinity of the Kings River. Although there had been rumors of a great canyon in the area which rivaled Yosemite, no one had yet described it to the outside world. When Brewer's party finally came into the canyon, they were stunned—it was almost as spectacular as Yosemite, though it lacked waterfalls and monolithic cliffs. In the area of Kings Canyon they made several climbs, and members of the Survey immediately named one of these peaks Mt. Brewer. From its summit they saw a very high peak to the southeast. Thinking that it must be the highest point in the range (Mt. Dana had already been discredited), King and Cotter longed for it, and their epic five-day trek, described in a later chapter, was the first time in America's history that such mountainous and inhospitable terrain had been traversed.

A few weeks later members of the Survey crossed the range at Kearsarge Pass and dropped down into the Owens Valley. Although they visited a few more areas that summer, this is the last we hear of the Whitney Survey, for it soon completed its work and disbanded.

In the next few years many travelers came to the mountains to see the great canyons and big trees that had been gaining notoriety. One of these visitors was John Muir, who arrived in Yosemite Valley in 1868 for a brief stay. The following year he became a supervisor of sheepherders, a job that left him much free time to study the landscape. During the next few years Muir became a self-educated expert on the ecology of the Sierra. While in Tuolumne Meadows in 1869, he made the first ascent of the sharp and beautiful Cathedral Peak—this involved some difficult climbing of a nature not yet seen in this country. Although his mountaineering exploits are not as well known as his later geological theories, descriptive writings, and long struggles to exclude sheep and lumbermen from his beloved mountains, Muir's solo ascents of Mt. Ritter, Mt. Whitney, and many other peaks (mentioned only obliquely in his writings) place him among the first rank of early American mountaineers.

Though much country had been explored by the early 1890s, there were many blanks on the maps, and relatively few peaks had been climbed. Yet, remarkably, someone had already envisioned a trail stretching the length of the range. The idea had come to Theodore Solomons in 1884, when as a youth he had been herding cattle in the Central Valley and had been overwhelmed by a view of the Sierra on a pristine day. During the early 1890s Solomons set out summer after summer, seeking the most feasible path for his "high mountain route." Although he is best remembered for his explorations around the headwaters of the San Joaquin

River and for many of the place names he bestowed in this area, the John Muir Trail, begun in 1915, is perhaps his greatest legacy to the Sierra.

Another important figure of this era was Joseph N. LeConte, the son of a famous geologist who had visited Muir in Yosemite in 1870. Barely five feet in height, "Little Joe" explored watersheds, climbed many peaks, made a splendid set of photographs, and drew the first accurate maps of much of the Sierra. Like Solomons, LeConte was a charter member of the Sierra Club, which had been founded in 1892. His maps, distributed to club members, materially contributed to further exploration of the range. Club outings, which began in 1901 under the leadership of William Colby, brought more and more people into the mountains, in keeping with the club's by-laws "to render accessible the mountain regions."

James Hutchinson was the next prominent figure in the history of Sierra mountaineering. He was already 32 when, in 1899, he made his initial Sierra first ascent. During the next 20 years he compiled the most enviable first-ascent record any Sierra climber will ever have. A partial list of his peaks includes Matterhorn Peak, Mt. Mills, Mt. Abbot, Mt. Humphreys, North Palisade, and Black Kaweah.

Of all the men who have ever climbed in the Sierra, none was so legendary as Norman Clyde. A scholar of the classics, Clyde migrated west in the early part of the century, teaching at rural schools, but never staying in one place for very long. He seems to have been born with wanderlust. Clyde worked on his master's degree at Berkeley for a few years but dropped out over a dispute in curriculum. The following summer he made two first ascents in Yosemite. A curious gap of six years followed, but in 1920 he began to totally dominate the climbing history of the range. He moved to the east side of the Sierra in 1924 to become principal of the high school in Independence. He was 40 years old in the summer of 1925 and later wrote, "I sometimes think I climbed enough peaks this summer to render me a candidate for a padded cell—at least some people look at the matter in that way.'" In 1927, Clyde was involved in a Halloween scandal when he fired shots over the heads of pranksters who were trying to intimidate him. It was not thought proper for a high school principal to behave in such a manner, so Clyde left that job and for the next 40 years worked at odd jobs in the mountains, climbing at every opportunity. It is thought that he made over a thousand ascents in the range; his first ascents and new routes number around 130. If, as someone has said, the mark of a true mountaineer is his willingness to repeat climbs, then Clyde qualifies as few others are ever likely to do. He had many favorite peaks and would climb them year after year—he apparently ascended Mt. Thompson 50 times.

Clyde was famous for his huge packs, and it was a rare day when one would weigh less than 90 pounds. Guns, axes, cast-iron pots, and books in Greek all contributed to his monstrous Trapper Nelson. Although Clyde did his last new route in 1946, he attended Sierra Club Base Camps and High Trips in the capacity of woodcutter and guide until 1970, when he retired at the age of 85. Two years later he died in Big Pine.

In 1931 Robert L.M. Underhill, an East Coast mountaineer well-versed in the school of European rope management, came to California at the invitation of Francis Farquhar, an early climber and later a respected Sierra historian. The two had met the previous summer in Canada, and Farquhar thought it would be a good idea if Californians learned something about proper rope techniques. The pair gathered a small group of interested and talented climbers and went on a grand tour of the Sierra. Several fine first ascents resulted and a new age of California climbing began. Rockclimber-mountaineers such as Raffi Bedayn, Dave Brower, Glen Dawson, Jules Eichorn, Richard Leonard, and Hervey Voge put up scores of difficult routes in Yosemite Valley and the High Sierra during the 1930s. These routes were of a standard little dreamed of by Muir, LeConte, or

Hutchinson, involving high-angle rock and elaborate rope techniques to safeguard the participants. Few of the climbs in the High Sierra required a rope, but the confidence gained from the teachings of Underhill was invaluable. Leonard later wrote that if he were to fall, his first thought would be, "What would Underhill say of my technique?"

During the years after World War II most of the noteworthy climbing in the range was done by members of the Sierra Club outing groups. Since many of the peaks had already been ascended, the emphasis was on new routes on a multitude of virgin ridges and faces.

Rockclimbers "discovered" the big walls of the Sierra in the late 1950s. At first only the most prominent faces were climbed: Mt. Whitney's true east face in 1959, the southwest face of Mt. Conness in 1959, and the great east wall of Keeler Needle the following year. The leader of the last two climbs was the legendary Yosemite climber, Warren Harding. By the late 1960s hidden walls had been ferreted out, and though these were usually not more than 1,000 feet high, they were steep and difficult.

– Steve Roper

Overview of Climbs by Difficulty

Mt. Russell, East Ridge, (3rd class)
This is probably the best 3rd class ridge in the Sierra. Either climb it as a route or use it as a descent after climbing Fishhook Arête.

Mountaineer's Route (3rd class)
With just a bit of 4th class at the top, this is a moderate passage to Whitney's summit that avoids the crowds of the Whitney Trail while delivering that big mountain feeling.

Laurel Mountain, Northeast Gully (5.2)
This scramble is more about the location and views than the climbing quality. In the mile of mostly 3rd and 4th class rock there are a few 5th class moves. This route is usually soloed.

Bear Creek Spire, Northeast Ridge (5.5)
Some feel this climb is as classic as the North Arête. The climbing is mostly 3rd and 4th class, but there are a few 5th class

moves. Most confident Sierra climbers who can handle big exposure solo the route.

Tenaya Peak, Northwest Buttress (5.5, 14 pitches)

This is the Royal Arches of Tuolumne with endless amounts of fun moderate climbing in a spectacular setting.

Cathedral Peak (5.6, 5 pitches)

Incredibly popular for good reason: good rock, moderate climbing, and an incredible summit.

Mt. Conness, North Ridge (5.6)

If Cathedral Peak is the best intro peak climb, this is the best intro mountain climb. Mostly 4th class with occasional 5th class moves in a great position.

Mt. Conness, West Ridge (5.6, 12 pitches)

The best 5.6 mountain climb in the High Sierra. Mostly moderate moves and relatively straightforward. Easy to bypass exposure and harder moves if necessary.

Matthes Crest, Traverse from South to North (5.7)

One of the more unique rock formations anywhere. Mostly 4th class with a few sections of either 5th class moves or big exposure.

Matterhorn Peak (5.7, 6 pitches)

An aesthetic peak with a huge approach and mediocre climbing. The full High Sierra experience at only moderate technical difficulty.

Mt. Whitney, East Face (5.7, 13 pitches)

A wandering journey up mostly 3rd and 4th class terrain with a few memorable pitches of exposure and technical difficulty.

Mt. Whitney, East Buttress (5.7, 11 pitches)

This route is about the same difficulty and quality as the East Face. The climbing is more sustained but still rarely has a crux longer than 20 feet.

Temple Crag, Venusian Blind (5.7, 12 pitches)

This is one of the more moderate and quality arêtes on Temple Crag. The climb is long and exposed with a few technical sections between arête and ridge scrambling.

Temple Crag, Moon Goddess Arête (5.8, 14 pitches)

Similar to Venusian Blind, this route ascends an exposed arête with a few technical sections separated by fun scrambling.

Charlotte Dome, South Face (5.8, 12 pitches)

This is a favorite Sierra climb for many people. The climbing is sustained and on exceptional rock reminiscent of Tuolumne.

Bear Creek Spire, North Arête (5.8, 10 pitches)

This is one of the more accessible Sierra peaks and fast teams often climb it car-to-car in a day. The first half of the route ascends a striking and steep arête while the second half is a scramble up an enjoyable and exposed ridge.

Eichorn's Pinnacle, West Pillar (5.9, 5 pitches)

This is a more challenging and less crowded way to get to the most striking summit in Tuolumne, if not the entire High Sierra.

Mt. Russell, Fishhook Arête (5.9, 8 pitches)

A combination of size, rock quality, and the striking arête make this a must-do for experienced Sierra climbers. Once you see the route from the summit of Mt. Whitney, you will be compelled to climb it.

Mt. Goode, North Buttress (5.9, 9 pitches)

The relatively straightforward approach, beautiful setting and steep, dramatic buttress add to the appeal of this route.

Temple Crag, Sun Ribbon Arête (5.10a, 18 pitches)

This is one of the longest and most classic arêtes in the High Sierra and offers a rare opportunity for a Tyrolean Traverse. You must move fast on this one.

Third Pillar of Dana, Regular Route (5.10b, 5 pitches)

Four pitches of good climbing lead to what is probably the best finishing pitch of any High Sierra climb.

Incredible Hulk, Red Dihedral, (5.10b, 11 pitches)

The Incredible Hulk has probably the best rock in the High Sierra and the Red Dihedral is its most classic 5.10 route. This climb is long, sustained, and amazing.

following pages: The stunning Whitney Crest glows in post-thunderstorm light. (PatitucciPhoto)

Mt. Conness, Southwest Face (5.10c, 9 pitches)

This climb looks like a true alpine big wall both from a distance, from the base, and when you are on it. The climbing is mostly 5.8 and 5.9 with a few distinct 5.10 cruxes.

Keeler Needle, Harding Route (5.10c, 13 pitches)

This is the coolest-looking formation in the High Sierra but the rock is not as good as it looks. A huge and adventurous climb.

Incredible Hulk, Positive Vibrations (5.11a, 13 pitches)

Probably the best route in the High Sierra. Long and sustained with perfect rock. It doesn't get any better.

Incredible Hulk, Sun Spot Dihedral (5.11b, 12 pitches)

More sustained and almost as classic as Positive Vibrations. Long endurance pitches with occasional technical cruxes.

High Sierra Climbing Beta

High Sierra Climbing Skills

You need a solid base of trad climbing skills to lead a High Sierra route. Most climbs will involve a little bit of every technique from face climbing and stemming to hand cracks and the occasional chimney. Build confidence with these techniques on multi-pitch climbs at a granite area like Tuolumne Meadows, Yosemite Valley, or Lover's Leap.

When choosing a climb, keep in mind that in the High Sierra, most climbers lead at least a number grade lower than their cragging ability. For example, if you lead 5.9 trad at the crags, you will probably only be comfortable leading 5.8 or even 5.7 in the High Sierra. This is because you are generally weaker at high altitude, but also because you must not fall on Sierra climbs. Because of the ledgy terrain, even short falls are serious and rescue is usually at least a day away

High Sierra Non-Climbing Skills

Technical climbing skills are only a small requirement for High Sierra routes. Routefinding skills, hiking fitness, and general mountain sense are just as important. Approaches typically involve at least a few miles of hiking off a main

trail. Our *High Sierra Climbing* guidebook features the most detailed info ever provided for these approaches. However, you will still need some basic orienteering skills to navigate through cross-country sections. Also, High Sierra climbs ascend complex and confusing terrain that demands careful attention to the topo and some intuition. Important tip: on the approach, keep the topo handy and study the route from a distance. Do not wait until you are at the base to look at the topo. At that point, much of the upper route will probably be hidden and it may be hard to orient yourself. Almost all climbs require a substantial approach at high elevation. If out of shape, you may be too tired to climb by the time you reach the base of the route. All *High Sierra Climbing* routes can be climbed car-to-car in a day by a fast team. Most parties, however, will prefer to camp near the base, therefore you will need all the requisite backcountry camping skills.

Climbing Gear

Climb light. Carrying a heavy pack and rack at altitude will slow you down and, more importantly, remove the fun. Carry only what you need (but don't skimp on food, water, and a rain shell).

The typical rack includes: one 9-10mm rope, 1 set of nuts, 1-2 sets of cams .6-3", 10 slings, 20 lightweight carabiners, belay device, lightweight harness. For the High Sierra, slings are better than quickdraws because they are more versatile. On a wandering pitch you will want a sling on every piece to reduce rope drag and on straight up and down pitches you can convert your slings into make-shift quickdraws. 50m ropes are preferred because they are lighter than 60m ropes and after 50m it is usually impossible to communicate with the belayer. (All the topos in the *High Sierra Climbing* guidebook are set for 50m ropes, but we tell you where you can link pitches with a 60m rope). A retreat rope may be helpful for some climbs. However, sometimes it is better to rappel with just one rope because long rappels in the High Sierra often result in stuck ropes or pulling loose blocks down on yourself.

Non-Climbing Gear

Sun hat, sunscreen, sunglasses, warm hat, water-resistant lightweight jacket (don't bring a heavy Gore-Tex jacket), water filter or iodine tablets, and a pencil (so you can make comments and suggestions on the SuperTopos and send us feedback!). Don't forget the trekking poles! These indispensable companions will save your knees and help you move faster. They also make a great "rudder" when glissading. Get the lightweight kind that collapse really small (we like Leki poles). Also, hike in using lightweight approach shoes. Remember, you climb carrying your approach shoes so don't bring heavy hiking boots. Definitely bring a headlamp (lightweight LED models are best). An ice axe and crampons may be necessary for climbs on Temple Crag.

For a good backcountry camping gear list, visit the Sierra Mountain Center web site: www.sierramountaincenter.com.

Altitude Sickness

It takes a few days for most people to adjust to the rarefied air. Not to mention, climbing at altitude makes everything feel much harder. Drink lots of water and don't run around too fast if you're just coming up from low elevations. It's a good idea to camp at least one night at the trailhead and a better idea to spend a few days cragging at high elevation. Tuolumne Meadows is the best place for high altitude cragging. If you can't make it there check out Rock Creek for awesome granite trad and sport climbs at the Main Attraction Wall and Iris Slabs.

If you do get a bad headache or feel nauseous, the best cure is to head to lower elevation.

Thunderstorms and Lightning Strikes

The High Sierra has some of the best weather of any alpine rock climbing area on earth. That said, note that the High Sierra is still in a massive mountain range and receives severe thunderstorms and lightning throughout the summer. Check the weather before you climb and scope the retreat route beforehand. Most thunderstorms originate from the west, so if you are climbing an east-facing route, you may not see thunderstorms until they are on top of you. Always carry a rain shell.

Lightning tends to hit high points, trees, and water, but will hit low points next to high rocks, flat areas near tall trees, and dry land in areas with lakes. Know how to perform CPR. Unlike with nearly any other type of injury that stops the heart, electrical shock victims can suddenly respond even after extended CPR, so CPR should be continued indefinitely.

Current Road and Weather

Your best bet is to check the general High Sierra Weather: http://www.weather.com/weather/local/USCA0661

Getting There

Air Travel

Reno/Tahoe Airport is the closest airport to most High Sierra climbs. From there, you will need to rent a car and drive 2-3.5 hours to your climbing destination. You can also fly into Los Angeles, Oakland, San Francisco, Sacramento, or Fresno. Each of these places requires a 5-7 hour drive to the East Side.

Bus Travel

The Eastern Sierra has little bus service or public transportation. The only town that can be reached by bus is Mammoth Lakes via the **Mammoth Shuttle** (760-934-3030).

Car Travel

Almost all climbs are accessed by U.S. 395 and the small Eastern Sierra towns of Lone Pine, Independence, Big Pine, Bishop, Tom's Place, and Bridgeport.

Below are the general driving times (in hours) to the Eastern Sierra (times vary depending on which trailhead you are heading for).

Tuolumne Meadows: 1-3; Yosemite Valley: 2-4; Reno: 2-4; Los Angeles: 4-6; San Francisco: 5-7; Las Vegas: 4-6; Salt Lake City: 9-11; Boulder: 18-20.

Nearby Towns and Trailheads

Lone Pine and Whitney Portal Essentials

Nearby Peaks: Mt. Russell, Mt.Whitney
Groceries: Joseph's Bi-Rite Market

Restaurants: The **Pizza Factory** (301 South Main Street; 760-876-4707) has inexpensive pizza and salad bar. **Mt. Whitney Restaurant** (Corner of U.S. 395 and Whitney Portal Road; 760-876-5751) is open seven days a week and serves buffalo, ostrich, and veggie burgers. **Totem Cafe** (131 South Main Street; 760-876-1120) has American-style cuisine and patio dining. **Seasons Restaurant** (227 South Main Street; 760-876-8927) is pricey, but serves good food and large portions. **PJ's Bake and Broil** (446 South Main Street; 760-876-5796) is the classic diner in town. High Sierra Café at the south end of town is a good breakfast spot.

Services at Whitney Portal: Don't miss the hamburgers and french fries at the **Whitney Portal Store** (760-876-0030). The Whitney Portal Store also sells tourist stuff, maps, books, and they have a great deal on bear canisters, which you can also rent.

Trailhead Camping: It is often a good idea to camp at the Whitney Portal before starting your climb. You will get an early start on the hike and start acclimatizing (Whitney Portal is at 8,300 feet). There are ten walk-in sites near the trailhead (follow signs to "Hiker Overnight Camping") reserved for hikers/climbers that cost $6 a night and are first come, first served. You can also stay at the Whitney Portal Campground but will have to shell out $14 a night and reserve your site in advance. For more info: www.r5.fs.fed.us/inyo/vvc/cmpgrnds.htm#LonePine

Independence and Onion Valley Essentials

Nearby Peak: Charlotte Dome
Groceries: There is a small market in town but your best bet is to shop at Joseph's in Lone Pine or one of the three markets in Bishop.

Restaurants: Not much to choose from but the **Rocking Rhino** (123 North Edwards; 760-878-0052) has good pizza, beer, and a nice atmosphere.

Trailhead Camping: Onion Valley Campground is located at 9,200 feet, costs $11/night (reservations recommended; 877-444-6677) and has picnic tables and piped water.

Big Pine and Big Pine Creek Essentials

Nearby Peak: Temple Crag
Groceries: **Carroll's Market** and the **Mobil Station** are limited and have the only groceries in town. Stock up in Bishop, which is 15 miles north on U.S. 395.

Restaurants: **Uncle Bud's** (120 South Main Street) has pizzas, salads, and sandwiches and the **Country Kitchen** (181 South Main Street; 760-938-9917) serves diner breakfasts.

Services at Big Pine Creek: **Glacier Lodge** (11 miles west of U.S. 395; 760-938-2837) has cabins for $70/night that sleep two to nine people, a general store, and a restaurant. $4 showers are available between 10 a.m. and 4 p.m. **Glacier Pack Train** (0.5 mile east of Glacier Lodge; 760-938-2538) provides pack trips into the backcountry.

Trailhead Camping: Big Pine Creek Campground and Upper Sage Flat Campground are located along Glacier Lodge Road at 7,700 feet and have picnic tables, restrooms, and water. Both are $13/night (reservations recommended; 877-444-6677). If you are up for hiking in a mile to First Falls, there is a free walk-in campground with picnic tables, fire rings, and pit toilets (you must get your own water from the creek).

Bishop and South Lake Essentials

Nearby Peak: Mt. Goode
Groceries: Vons (North Main Street) is the gigantic grocery store located next to K-mart. Joseph's Bi-Rite Market is in the center of town, across from Kava, and Manor Market (3100 West Line Street) has a great beer and wine selection as well as a deli and basic groceries.

Restaurants and Cafes: **Spellbinder's Books** (124 South Main Street; 760- 873-4511) is not only a cool bookstore, but also serves great coffee at the coffee bar in the back of the store. **The Bishop Grill** (across from Wilson's Eastside Sports; 760-873-7248) serves greasy and tasty diner food—breakfast is great. **Jack's Waffle Shop** (437 North Main Street; 760-872-7971) and **Inyo Country Store** (177 Academy Street) also serve breakfast. **Kava** (next to Wilson's; 760-872-1010) is the local climber hang and serves coffee and tasty scones and muffins. **Schat's Bakkery** (763 North Main Street; 760-873-7156) has every type of pastry and excellent sandwiches and bread. **Western Thai Kitchen** (930 North Main Street; 760-872-3246) serves tasty Thai food as well as burgers and fries—a local favorite. For Mexican food there are three options: At **Amigos** (285 North Main Street; 760-872-2189) try the carne asada, **Taqueria Las Palmas** (136 East Line Street; 760-873-4337) has awesome burritos, and **La Casita** (175 South Main Street; 760-873-4828) has okay food and a full bar (that means margaritas!). **Whiskey Creek** (524 North Main Street; 760-873-7174) has a great bar with yummy salads, pub food, and a sit-down dining room with fancier choices such as filet mignon and ahi tuna. **Upper Crust Pizza** (1180 North Main Street; 760-872-8153) has some of the best pizza we've tasted—try the "Illusian."

Other: **The Rubber Room** (175-B North Main Street; 888-395-ROCK) is the best place anywhere for quality resoles. There is a Bank of America, Washington Mutual, and Union Bank of California in town. The **Bishop Twin Theatre** (237 North Main Street; 760-873-3575) has two screens and new movies weekly. **Mountain Light Gallery** (106 South Main Street; 760-873-7700) features the incredible work of Galen and Barbara Rowell and is definitely worth a visit.

Services at South Lake: There is a general store in Habbegers, which is 3 miles from Highway 168 on the way to South Lake.

Trailhead Camping: Willow Campground is located at 9,000 feet on the road to South Lake. Sites are $13/night. You'll need to get water from the creek.

Tom's Place and Rock Creek Essentials

Nearby Peak: Bear Creek Spire

Groceries: There is a little grocery store at Tom's Place, but for major groceries head 20 minutes south to Bishop or 15 minutes north to Mammoth Lakes. Bishop has three large stores and Mammoth Lakes has a Vons (off Old Mammoth Road).

Restaurants: **Tom's Place Resort** (right off U.S. 395) has lodging as well as a restaurant and bar (next to the store). For a more extensive selection, cruise down the grade to Bishop or up to Mammoth Lakes. In Mammoth the places to go are: **Roberto's Mexican Cafe** (271 Old Mammoth Road; 760-934-3667) for great Mexican food and strong margaritas, **Shogun** (452 Old Mammoth Road; 760-934-3970) for fresh sushi, **Good Life Cafe** (126 Old Mammoth Road; 760-934-1734) for healthy food, **Bergers** (6118 Minaret Road; 760-934-6622) for awesome burgers and fries.

Services at Rock Creek: **Rock Creek Lodge** (Rock Creek Road; 877-935-4170 or 760-935-4170) has a small store and a restaurant (known for its pies!)

Trailhead Camping: Mosquito Flat Trailhead Campground is a free walk-in campground only for persons with an overnight backcountry permit for the following day, and the stay limit is only one night. The campground is located across the bridge that leads to Eastern Brook Lakes. There are 12 other campgrounds to choose from between Tom's Place and Mosquito Flat that cost around $15 a night. Most of these campgrounds do not require reservations.

For more information, visit: www.rockcreeklake.com/camping/

Tuolumne Meadows/Lee Vining Essentials

Nearby Peaks: Mt. Conness, Third Pillar of Dana, Cathedral Peak, Matthes Crest

Groceries: A limited selection of high-priced groceries are available at the Tuolumne Meadows store. In addition, you can purchase groceries in Lee Vining at the Lee Vining Market. Mammoth has a large Vons supermarket.

Restaurants: The **Tuolumne Meadows Grill** serves hamburgers, fries, etc., and has limited hours. The **Tuolumne Lodge** has a restaurant that serves breakfast and dinner in the middle part of summer. Eight miles east of Tuolumne Meadows, the **Tioga Pass Resort** houses a cozy dining room with good food. The **Mobil Gas Station,** located 14 miles from Tuolumne Meadows in Lee Vining, serves some of the best food in the area. This isn't just any gas station—its deli has a great selection of sandwiches, pizzas, fish tacos, and a variety of other savory treats for breakfast, lunch, and dinner.

Camping: There is one campground in Tuolumne Meadows located next to the Tuolumne Store that has about 300 sites. Half of the sites can be reserved in advance at http://reservations.nps.gov/ (reserve them at least 2-3 months in advance) and half of the sites are on a first come, first served basis (arrive in the morning to ensure you get a site). Sites cost $18 per night with a six-person two-car limit. Mosquitoes can be particularly fierce so bring bug spray and bug netting. Bears regularly break into cars with food in them so use bear boxes.

Located 7 to 10 miles east of Tuolumne Meadows are five Forest Service campgrounds, many of which are first come, first served. These campgrounds are often battered by icy winds. Twelve miles east of Tuolumne Meadows, the Lee Vining Creek campground is not only sheltered from the wind, it's set next to a beautiful trout-stocked creek. You will pay $8 per night on a first come, first served basis. Along Highway 120 toward Yosemite Valley are several additional campgrounds requiring moderate to long drives. The campground reservation office in Tuolumne has information on current campground conditions.

There are two free camping areas near Mono Lake:

1) 2.2 miles below Conway Summit at the north end of the guardrail at the huge turn. Can be tricky to find a perfectly flat spot. Great view of Mono Lake. The Buttermilk-looking boulders nearby actually have terrible rock.

2) Black Point: From Lee Vining, head north on U.S. 395 for about 5 miles to Cemetery Road. Drive 3.3 miles on Cemetery Road (mostly dirt road, low clearance okay) and take a right on the road that leads to Black Point. When there is an option, stay right.

Lodges and Cabins: In addition to campsites, there are more plush accommodations available in Tuolumne and the High Sierra, including the Tuolumne Meadows Lodge, White Wolf, and the High Sierra Camps (www.yosemitepark.com/html/accommodation.html). Just outside of the park boundary is the Tioga Pass Resort (www.tiogapassresort.com), which offers cabins year-round (in the winter you need to ski or snowmobile up to them). Drive 15 miles east from Tuolumne Meadows and you will reach Lee Vining, a small town with a few motels, restaurants, and other basic services.

Bridgeport and Twin Lakes Essentials

Nearby Peaks: Incredible Hulk, Matterhorn Peak

Groceries: There's a small market.

Restaurants: **Hays Street Café** (21 Hays Street; 760-932-7141) is a great breakfast and lunch spot (it is a little pricey). There are a few decent burger spots, too.

Services at Twin Lakes: The **Twin Lakes Resort** (760-932-7751) has a small store and a restaurant that serves great burgers.

Trailhead Camping:

Mono Village Campground: (760-932-7071) at 7,100 feet is $12/night.

Lower Twin Lakes Campground: (760-932-7070) at 7,000 feet and $10/night.

Honeymoon Flat Campground: (760-932-7070) at 7,000 feet and $10/night.

Hot Springs: 0.25 mile south of town on U.S. 395 turn east onto Jack Sawyer Road. When the paved road veers right after a few hundred yards, continue straight on a dirt road for less than a mile to its end. The tubs are paved and clean but often crowded.

When to Climb

Almost everyone climbs in the High Sierra between June and October. From November through April, the High Sierra is pounded with snow from big Pacific storms.

Note: Below, the snow conditions are listed for an average snow year. Most snow years are not average and the projections below will be way off if it has been a heavy or light snow year. Your best bet is to search online for your climb on the SuperTopo Route Beta page to check current conditions. If there is nothing there, ask a question in the SuperTopo Forum.

Summer thunderstorm near Bishop. (Jody Langford)

May – Only in low snow years will climbs be easily accessible. In general, most of the approaches will be snow-covered and many of the access roads may not be plowed. May is mostly dry but expect a few storms. There are no crowds in May.

June – Aside from a rare storm, June is usually dry with warm temps and nice long days. Most of the access roads are plowed, but there will still be snow on most approaches. Thunderstorms begin to develop so keep a close eye on the weather. The crowds start showing at the end of June, and it becomes more competitive to get overnight camping permits. Charlotte Dome and Temple Crag are usually the first climbs to access easily.

July and August – Prime Sierra climbing weather. Temperatures are hot at the trailheads, but perfect on the climbs. This is also prime thunderstorm season so watch the weather closely. There are crowds, and it is competitive for overnight camping permits (get reservations at least a month in advance).

September – Still great climbing conditions, but the nights are cool. Some north-facing routes may be uncomfortably cold in the shade. The crowds start to thin.

October – Shorter days and cold nights mean less people. Climbing in the shade is no fun. Weather is mostly dry, but the first winter storm can arrive late in the month. Easy to get overnight camping permits.

November – Frigid nights and short days keep most people out of the High Sierra. Winter storms begin to arrive more frequently. A rare time to get some solitude before the heavy snow sets in.

December-April – Got skis? Frequent winter storms and icy temperatures make the High Sierra only accessible to those that enjoy suffering. In exceptionally dry years, during a warm spell, you may be able to run up one of the peaks in a day in December.

Camping and Permits

Backcountry Camping Permits

When camping in the backcountry, you need a permit, which can be picked up at one of the ranger stations listed below (sorry, no mail order permits). A quota system is in place in the summer and fall, which means only a limited number of permits are issued each day. Of this number, 25-40 percent are available on a walk-in basis for free at the ranger station and 60-75 percent of the permits can be reserved in advance for a $3-10 fee. Most of the classic Sierra climbs are accessed off popular trails where permits are in high demand, especially from June to August. During this time, you may need to reserve your permit more than a month in advance. If you show up for a walk-in permit, you may be denied.

Ranger Stations

Inyo National Forest (760-873-2483)
Popular peaks: Mt. Whitney, Mt. Russell, Temple Crag, Palisades, Mt. Goode, Bear Creek Spire, Laurel Mountain, Clyde Minaret.

Mt. Whitney Ranger Station (640 South Main Street, Lone Pine; 760-876-6200)

White Mountain Ranger Station (798 North Main Street, Bishop; 760-873-2500)

Mammoth Ranger Station (2500 Main Street, Mammoth Lakes; 760-924-5500)

Mono Basin Scenic Area Visitor Center (On U.S. 395, Lee Vining; 760-647-3044)

Tuolumne Wilderness Center (Highway 120, in parking lot 0.25 mile from ranger station; 209-372-0740, www.nps.gov/yose/wilderness/permits.htm)

Toiyabe National Forest/Hoover Wilderness
Popular Peaks: Matterhorn Peak, Incredible Hulk

Bridgeport Ranger Station (On U.S. 395, 0.25 mile south of Bridgeport; 760-932-7070)

Kings Canyon National Park
Popular Peak: Charlotte Dome

Road's End Wilderness Permit Station (located at Road's End; 559-565-3708)

Climbing Guides and Climbing Gear

Sierra Mountain Center (174 West Line Street, Bishop; 760-873-8526) is the best guiding service in the Eastern Sierra. They guide just about every classic climb in the High Sierra and every climb contained in the *High Sierra Climbing* SuperTopo guidebook. Their cool web site: www.sierramountaincenter.com is loaded with photos, route descriptions, slide shows, and extensive gear lists for most classic High Sierra climbs.

There are two great climbing shops on the East Side that have everything you need for any climbing or backpacking adventure: **Wilson's Eastside Sports** (224 North Main Street, Bishop; 760-873-7520) and **Mammoth Mountaineering** (437 Old Mammoth Road, Mammoth Lakes; 760-934-4191).

Bears

Every year the bears seem to get smarter and more aggressive. If you do not take precautions, YOUR CAR WILL BE BROKEN INTO. Bears are active both at the trailhead parking areas and popular camping areas in the backcountry.

Bears at the Trailhead Parking Areas

While the Whitney and Onion Valley Trailheads currently have the worst problems, all Sierra trailheads experience bear break-ins. If you have any food or anything smelling like food in your car, it will be broken into. If you are lucky, they break a window. If you are unlucky, they will peel the upper part of the door down causing thousands of dollars in body damage to your car. However, even if your car is free of food, a bear may break into it just because he sees enough clutter (bags, backpacks, clothes, etc). For this reason, it is essential to clear out your car as much as possible before you reach the trailhead and put any loose items in the trunk. Make the car look empty. Food lockers are provided at the trailhead, but they are often full and not always secure so don't plan on using them for more than a night.

Bears in the Backcountry

A bear's natural habitat is the forests and shrublands below 8,000 feet (2,438 meters), but they will frequently roam above these elevations in order to steal food from backpackers. Don't even think about "bear

Sarah Felchlin

bagging" your food (the bears figured this one out) or sleeping with your food (a backpacker has been mauled by a bear). The only way to protect your food is in a bear canister. These large black plastic containers are bulky, heavy, and a pain in the ass to deal with. However, they are also the only way to protect your food from bears and are mandatory in many popular backcountry areas. Bear canisters can be rented for between $5 and $10 per week from any ranger station, as well as at the Whitney Portal Store. To own a bear canister, you will need to fork over $80 at a ranger station or you can get one for the great price of $57.25 (shipped) from the Whitney Portal Store.

Marmots and Mosquitos

Above 11,000 feet, the marmots are more of a problem than the bears. These fury little critters act cute, but if you drop your guard for a minute they will devour your food with the grace and speed of a garbage disposal. Hang all of your food and anything scented (toothpaste, sunscreen, garbage) from a large boulder or, better yet, bring a bear canister (for rent at the ranger stations).

During a one-month period around June and July, the mosquitos are so dense that even repellent may not prevent bites. Their arrival varies from year to year, area to area, and depends on the snow year. Come prepared (especially if you are camping) with long pants, long sleeves, and DEET repellant. Ask rangers and the SuperTopo Forum about current mosquito conditions.

East Side Summer Cragging Areas

First-rate cragging abounds on the East Side. It is a good idea to crag at high elevation before climbing a High Sierra route to both acclimatize and get comfortable on Sierra granite. The areas listed below are between 8,000 and 10,000 feet and are climbable from May–October. There are a number of other crags and boulders at lower elevations, such as the Buttermiks, Happy Boulders, and Owens River Gorge. These areas are too hot in the summer.

Whitney Portal: Great climbing…if you climb 5.10 or harder. The rock and lines are as good as Yosemite and present a mixture of splitter cracks and face moves on 80-degree, white granite walls. The season is spring and fall, but unfortunately there is not a good guidebook to the area.

Cardinal Pinnacle: Another great area… if you climb 5.10 or harder. The fine-grained granite has numerous edges and splitter cracks. The routes are all three to four pitches and end on a cool summit. The guidebook is *Bishop Area Rock Climbs* by Marty Lewis.

Rock Creek/Iris Slab: Rock Creek has excellent (hard) bouldering along the river and super fun sport climbs on perfect granite edges (there are not many routes under 5.10). Iris Slab has more easy and moderate climbs. The guidebook is *Bishop Area Rock Climbs* by Marty Lewis.

Dike Wall and Crystal Crag: Located above beautiful alpine lakes and easily accessed, the Dike Wall has excellent sport climbs that are 5.10 and up. Crystal Crags has more moderate climbs also of excellent quality. The guidebook is *Eastern Sierra Summer* by Mick Ryan available at www.Rockfax.com.

Bear Creek Spire rises above Mack Lake. (Jody Langford)

SuperTopo Mission

- Help climbers ascend and descend routes quickly, efficiently, and safely by creating the most accurate and informative climbing topos ever published.

- Capture the mystery, adventure, and humor of climbing by publishing the histories, anecdotes, and outrageous stories of each route.

- Promote clean climbing by publishing the most up-to-date rack info as well as hammerless ratings for each pitch.

- Stress the importance of low impact climbing and promote stewardship of the environment.

Visit www.SuperTopo.com Before Each Climb

There is much more beta available for free on the SuperTopo web site: www.supertopo.com. This information may be more current than the beta available here.

The web site offers additional free beta for each climb:

- photo galleries
- trip reports
- route condition updates
- closures and rockfall warnings
- route beta email alerts

The web site is packed with general High Sierra info:

- free downloadable color topos
- road and weather conditions
- everything you need to know about staying in the High Sierra
- good routes for first-time High Sierra climbers
- general trip planning info

Free Climbing Ratings

USA (Yosemite Decimal System)	UIAA	France	UK	Australia
5.1	I	1	M	4
5.2	II	2	D	6
5.3	III	2+	3A/3B VD	8
5.4	III+ / IV	3-	3B/3C HVD	
5.5	IV+	3		10
5.6	V-	3+	3C/4A S · 4A/4B HS	12
5.7	V	4	4A/4C VS	14
5.8	V+	4+		16
5.9	VI-	5	4C/5B HVS	
5.10a	VI	5+		18
5.10b	VI+	6A	5A/5C E1	19
5.10c	VII-	6A+	5B/6A E2	20
5.10d	VII	6B	5C/6A E3	21
5.11a	VII+	6B+		
5.11b	VIII-	6C		22
5.11c		6C+	6A/6B E4	23
5.11d	VIII	7A		24
5.12a	VIII+	7A+	6A/6C E5	
5.12b	IX-	7B		25
5.12c	IX	7B+	6B/6C E6	26
5.12d		7C		27
5.13a	IX+	7C+		28
5.13b	X-	8A	6C/7A E7	29
5.13c	X	8A+		30
5.13d		8B	6C/7A E8	31
5.14a	X+	8B+		32
5.14b	XI-	8C	7A/7B E9	33
5.14c	XI	8C+		34
5.14d	XI+	9A	7A/7B E10	35
5.15a		9A+		36

Cam Sizes by Brand

Ref Size*	BD Camalots	CCH Aliens	Metolius Cams	Trango Big Bros	Wild Country Friends
0.4"	.1 red	.33 black	00 gray		
0.5"	.2 yellow	.375 blue	0 purple		0 red
0.6"	.3 purple	.5 green	1 blue		.5 orange
0.75"	.4 gray	.75 yellow	2 yellow		1 yellow
1"	.5 pink	1 red	3 orange		1.25 brown
1.25"	.75 green	1.5 orange	4 red		1.5 sky
1.5"	1 red	2 purple	5 black		2 pink
1.75"	1 red	2.5 gray	6 green		2.5 royal
2"	2 yellow	2.5 gray	7 blue		3 navy
2.5"	2 yellow		8 purple		3.5 purple
3"	3 blue		9 burgundy		4 black
3.5"	3.5 gray		10 dark blue		4 black
3.5-4.5"	4 purple			1 red	5 silver
4.5-5.5"	4.5 red			2	
5.5-7"	5 green			3 green	6 plum
7-8"				3 green	
8-12"				4 blue	

*"Ref size" is the optimal crack width for a given camming unit. It is not the range given by the manufacturer.

Understanding the Maps

Topo Symbols

Right-facing corner		Roof	Bolt x
Left-facing corner		Ledge	Rappel anchor
		Slab ///;	
Straight-in crack		Belay station ❶	Face climbing
Groove		Pitch length 130'●	Pine tree
Arête			Oak-like tree
Flake		Optional belay ○	Bush
			Knob O
Chimney		False belay ⊘	Hole ●

Notes on Rack

• "nuts" refers to any nut, stopper, or chock. "micro"= #1, 2; "sml"= #3-5; "med"= #6-8; "lrg"= #9-13
• for cams, "2 ea .75-1.5" means bring two sets of all sizes between .75" and 1.5". Check the cam size chart to see which cam corresponds to which crack size.

Notes on Topo

• "belay takes .6-1" means, while leading the pitch, save enough .6-1" cams and nuts to build a natural anchor.
• a number next to a tree is its height.

Topo Abbreviations

ow = offwidth
lb = lieback
p = fixed piton
R = runout (dangerous fall)

Metric System Conversions

1 inch = 2.54 centimeters
1 foot = 0.305 meters
100 feet = 30.5 meters
50 yards = 45.7 meters

Overview Graphics

Canyon Wall	
2WD/4WD dirt road	
Road or State Route	⑩
Federal Highway	⑩
Hikers' trail	
Climbers' trail	
Cross-country travel	

Star Ratings

★★★★★ - undisputed classic
★★★★ - excellent climb
★★★ - good climb
★★ - okay climb
★ - barely included in this book

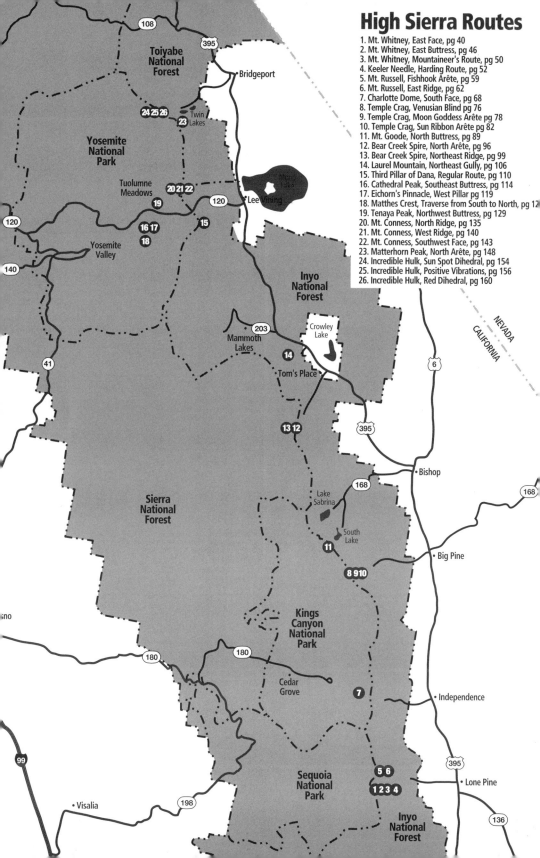

High Sierra Routes

1. Mt. Whitney, East Face, pg 40
2. Mt. Whitney, East Buttress, pg 46
3. Mt. Whitney, Mountaineer's Route, pg 50
4. Keeler Needle, Harding Route, pg 52
5. Mt. Russell, Fishhook Àrête, pg 59
6. Mt. Russell, East Ridge, pg 62
7. Charlotte Dome, South Face, pg 68
8. Temple Crag, Venusian Blind pg 76
9. Temple Crag, Moon Goddess Arête pg 78
10. Temple Crag, Sun Ribbon Arête pg 82
11. Mt. Goode, North Buttress, pg 89
12. Bear Creek Spire, North Arête, pg 96
13. Bear Creek Spire, Northeast Ridge, pg 99
14. Laurel Mountain, Northeast Gully, pg 106
15. Third Pillar of Dana, Regular Route, pg 110
16. Cathedral Peak, Southeast Buttress, pg 114
17. Eichorn's Pinnacle, West Pillar pg 119
18. Matthes Crest, Traverse from South to North, pg 12
19. Tenaya Peak, Northwest Buttress, pg 129
20. Mt. Conness, North Ridge, pg 135
21. Mt. Conness, West Ridge, pg 140
22. Mt. Conness, Southwest Face, pg 143
23. Matterhorn Peak, North Arête, pg 148
24. Incredible Hulk, Sun Spot Dihedral, pg 154
25. Incredible Hulk, Positive Vibrations, pg 156
26. Incredible Hulk, Red Dihedral, pg 160

Toiyabe National Forest

Bridgeport

Yosemite National Park

Twin Lakes

Tuolumne Meadows

Lee Vining

Yosemite Valley

Inyo National Forest

Crowley Lake

Mammoth Lakes

Tom's Place

Bishop

Sierra National Forest

Lake Sabrina

South Lake

Big Pine

Kings Canyon National Park

Cedar Grove

Independence

NEVADA
CALIFORNIA

Fresno

Sequoia National Park

Inyo National Forest

Lone Pine

Visalia

Mt. Whitney

Mt. Whitney (14,496') is not only the highest peak in the lower 48, it has a massive and compelling face with two of the most popular technical rock routes in the High Sierra. The face is so impressive that at first glance from the approach it appears to be the domain of 15-pitch 5.11 climbs. Fortunately, there are two surprisingly moderate routes: East Buttress and East Face. While it is the most popular peak in the High Sierra, the permit system is so restrictive that you will rarely see more than a few parties on a technical rock route.

Approach

Start at Whitney Portal, about 20 minutes west of the town of Lone Pine. Take U.S. 395 and drive to the center of Lone Pine. At the traffic light, take the Whitney Portal Road west for 12 miles and park near the Mt. Whitney Trail trailhead.

The approach to the technical climbing routes is up the North Fork of Lone Pine Creek, far away from the standard Mt. Whitney Trail hikers take to the summit.

The approach from Whitney Portal to Iceberg Lake takes about 3 hours (double approach times if carrying a heavy pack). The approach is about 4 miles long, gains 4,300 feet in elevation, and is mostly on a well-defined climbers' trail. The trail is not always clear and a few exposed 3rd class sections make this trail only suitable for climbers and hikers with good routefinding skills.

From Whitney Portal to Lower Boy Scout Lake

The trail between Whitney Portal and Lower Boy Scout Lake is steep and often scorching hot from morning to early afternoon. Start hiking at dawn or in the late afternoon when it's in the shade or the heat will drain your energy.

Hike the Mt. Whitney Trail for about one mile to just before the North Fork of Lone

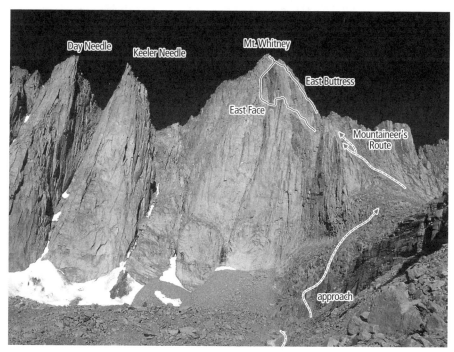

opposite: Mark Leffler on Mithral Dihedral, Mt Russell (5.10a). (PatitucciPhoto)

Keeler Needle

Mt. Whitney

East Face

East Buttress

Mountaineer's
Route

Whitney-
Russell Pass

Fishhook
Arête

Mt. Russell

East Ridge

Russell-Carillon
Pass

Iceberg Lake

Upper Boy
Scout Lake

Lower Boy
Scout Lake

Photo by Austin Post

Pine Creek (marked by a small wooden sign). Do not cross the creek. Take the well-defined climbers' trail on the right and climb steep dirt switchbacks through ferns and trees. Eventually the trail flattens and descends 50 feet to the first creek crossing under a tree canopy. Note: Between leaving the Mt. Whitney Trail and reaching Lower Boy Scout Lake, you only cross the creek twice,

Chris McNamara

both immediately after the only two places where the trail briefly loses elevation.

After the first creek crossing, continue out of the tree canopy on the south side of the creek, through some bush and talus to steep dirt switchbacks. After a while, the trail descends beneath an open slab, meets dense bushes/trees and immediately crosses the creek. (An off-route trail lures many

climbers up and left. If you accidentally go this way, don't worry, you will eventually regain the main approach around Lower Boy Scout Lake.) At this second crossing, the creek is divided into two fingers, and each requires stepping across slick rocks. The second finger passes under a beautiful (and drenching) 8-foot vertical waterfall and a very slick dead tree.

Pay attention—this next section is the first routefinding crux known as the Ebersbacher Ledges. Use this description along with the topo. After the second creek crossing, hike 200 feet along the rock wall on the north side of the creek and look for the first opportunity to scramble diagonally up and right on blocky and ledgy 3rd class. Climb 3rd class 70 feet to a distinct and solitary 30-foot-tall tree on a big ledge. Walk the ledge east (toward Lone Pine) for about 150 feet, move over a brief bulge, and continue east for another 150 feet (staying close to the wall and away from the edge). When the ledge starts continuously angling down, look for a passage up 30 feet of steep 3rd class. At the top, immediately move straight up and left toward the steep wall above (toward Whitney). Do not traverse above the slabs. Climb the steep switchbacks until directly under the steep wall and traverse west eventually reaching steep dirt switchbacks that lead to the outlet of Lower Boy Scout Lake.

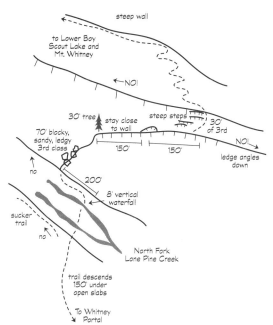

Approach from Lower Boy Scout Lake to just east of Upper Boy Scout Lake

Cross the outlet of Lower Boy Scout Lake (marked by "No Wood Fires" sign) and follow the south edge of Lower Boy Scout Lake and meadow to a short talus crossing (cross low). After the talus, a well-defined dirt climbers' trail gradually climbs up then turns to steep dirt switchbacks that end in another brief talus field. Cross the talus to dense bushes. A trail soon emerges that climbs steep switchbacks right of the talus and left of the dense bushes.

Pay attention—next comes the second routefinding crux of the approach. The switchbacks end in talus and you immediately look for a way to traverse right through bushes. In the next 100 yards, cross a few streams between a few short slabs and eventually traverse up right to the left ledge of a large open slab. This section is icy in the winter and slick with water in the summer. The next 100 yards climb the slab staying toward the left side. The slab eventually steepens for about 70 feet and a trail emerges and moves through bushes, and into a talus clearing below the last creek crossing (see photo below). Stop here and scout out the next section: Upper Boy Scout Lake is up and right (just out of view) and just left of Upper Boy Scout Lake are steep dirt switchbacks left of a series of progressively taller rock walls and pinnacles.

From the clearing, cross the stream through dense bushes and aim for the steep dirt switchbacks. Upper Boy Scout Lake will come into view once you are just above it. Note: Many climbers make the mistake of hiking to Upper Boy Scout Lake and continuing along its shores and up the prominent valley west of the lake.

Approach from just east of Upper Boy Scout Lake to the start of the climbs

Climb steep dirt switchbacks to a more gradual dirt trail. The dirt trail eventually vanishes into talus at a point where you get a dramatic view of the entire East Face of Mt. Whitney along with Keeler Needle and Day Needle. This next section is the third routefinding crux of the approach. Angle just slightly up the talus and look for a sandy trail that traverses a steep sandy slope beneath a wide cliff band. Pay attention—most people immediately take a steep trail up this dirt slope and immediately climb

The last creek crossing 100 yards below Upper Boy Scout Lake. This photo is taken 200 feet above the open slabs.

The start of the Mountaineer's descent as seen from 200 yards west of the summit. Notice the towers at right.

Chris McNamara

the cliff band on wet 3rd and 4th class. While this works, it is more dangerous and slower than the recommended way, which traverses more or less horizontally for a few hundred yards on a well-defined trail on the dirt slope. Eventually a clear trail of sandy switchbacks ascends the cliff band and shortly arrives at Iceberg Lake (last water source).

Final Approach for East Buttress & East Face

From 200 feet south of Iceberg Lake, locate the First and Second Towers and walk toward them. A steep trail eventually becomes intermittent trail and 3rd class then, just before the Second Tower, becomes just 3rd class. The start of the East Buttress Route is just below the Second Tower. For the East Face, continue up and left to a notch between the First Tower and Second Tower. Intense exposure signals the start of the East Face route.

Final Approach for Mountaineer's Route

Before starting, walk to the shore of Iceberg Lake and scope out the route. The photo on the route description page shows the start of the route better than can be described

here. From Iceberg Lake, stay left (south) of the main gully until you are forced into it.

Spring Conditions

Snow covers much of the approach into June, depending on the snow year. If the approach is covered with snow, you may not need an ice axe. However, you should hike early before the snow softens, or prepare for slushy snow and post-holing.

Descent

The Mountaineer's Route is the descent. It takes about 1-1.5 hours to get from the summit of Whitney to Iceberg Lake via the Mountaineer's Route. From the summit, stay near the edge and walk west 100 yards passing the metal cylindrical pit toilet. Then walk another 200 feet west to a steep gully with towers lining the right side (see photo above). Scramble down the left (west) side of the gully for 100 feet of steep 3rd class and then cross to the right (east) side of the gully. (If this section is icy in the early spring, you may be better off continuing down the left side of the gully and not crossing.) Follow the right side of the gully for a few hundred feet. Downclimb a short 3rd class section and immediately cut right through a notch. At this point, a trail emerges. Stay right and enter into the main Mountaineer's Route gully. Switchbacks lead down and gradually deteriorate into scree. When the gully starts to open up a little, stay to the right (if you stay left the gully steepens and turns into scree or snow). If you contour around, you will end up just below the start of each route (where you can pick up anything you left at the base). Continue down the climbers' trail and occasional ledges to Iceberg Lake.

Spring Conditions

Snow covers the Mountaineer's Route gully (between the summit and Iceberg Lake) usually until mid-June. The upper gully just below the summit is often icy and will require careful downclimbing and/or crampons and an ice axe. Lower, the main gully, because it receives early morning sun, is usually soft and perfect for glissading. An ice axe is recommended, but experienced glissaders, if they are careful, can get away with a ski pole or a rock. Snow in the gully makes the descent more dangerous and is only recommended if you have snow experience. It may also make the descent much faster and more fun.

Backcountry Camping

A few motivated people do the route car-to-car in a day. Most climbers, however, will want to camp at Upper Boy Scout Lake or Iceberg Lake the day before the climb. Start hiking early on day one and set up camp at Iceberg Lake (12,600 feet), climb on day two, and descend on day three. While this option means little hiking on the climbing day, hiking to Iceberg Lake is strenuous and it may be difficult for some people to sleep at this high elevation. The view, however, is incredible and you will have an opportunity to scope out the route and the descent.

Another option is to camp at Upper Boy Scout Lake (11,300 feet) where the temperatures are warmer and you are less likely to get altitude sickness. This will mean an additional 2-3 hours of hiking on the climbing day, but you will hike less distance with a heavy pack on the approach

and descent day. The downside: You can't see the routes from Upper Boy Scout Lake.

At either camping area, the marmots are aggressive and will scarf down all your food if you do not hang it from a boulder or, better yet, bring a bear canister (see "Bears" in Introduction). Also, human waste is a problem in the Whitney area and currently there is a voluntary pack-your-poop system.

If camping, you need a permit (see "Backcountry Camping Permits" in Introduction).

GPS Coordinates

Approach
Start of Mt. Whitney Trail:
    36° 35' 223", 118° 14' 409"
North Fork Lone Pine Creek:
    36° 35' 212", 118° 14' 722"
Just before first creek crossing:
    36° 35' 188", 118° 14' 952"
Just before second creek crossing:
    36° 35' 132", 118° 15' 152"
Top of Eberbacher's Ledges:
    36° 35' 165", 118° 15' 145"
Outlet of Lower Boy Scout Lake:
    36° 35' 082", 118° 15' 553"
After Lower Boy Scout Lake:
    36° 34' 978", 118° 15' 663"
After crossing talus, left of dense bushes
    and slabs: 36° 34' 972", 118° 15' 720"
Traverse right into bushes/slabs:
    36° 34' 860", 118° 15' 858"
Upper slabs: 36° 34' 876", 118° 16' 067"
Steep switchbacks above and south of
Upper Boy Scout Lake:
    36° 34' 775", 118° 16' 304"
Dramatic view of Mt. Whitney:
    36° 34' 688", 118° 16' 820"
Base of cliff before Iceberg Lake:
    36° 34' 710", 118° 17' 086"
200 feet south of Iceberg Lake:
    36° 34' 788", 118° 17' 088"
Summit of Mt. Whitney:
    36° 34' 709", 118° 17' 542"

Descent
Start of descent down Mountaineer's Route
(second gully to west):
    36° 34' 713", 118° 17' 615"
Main gully opens up and you move right
    (south): 36° 34' 788", 118° 17' 366"

East Face 5.7★★★★★

Time to climb route: **4-8 hours**

Approach time: **3-6 hours**

Descent time: **3-6 hours**

Sun exposure: **sunrise to early afternoon**

Height of route: **1,000'**

At first glance the 1,800-foot east face of Mt. Whitney appears much too difficult for a 5.7 route. Luckily, looks are deceiving and the face has just enough weaknesses that are connected in just the right ways to make the climbing mostly moderate and incredibly fun. The exposure and commitment are intense, making the route suitable for experienced 5.7 leaders.

The East Face is included in Steve Roper and Allen Steck's *50 Classic Climbs of North America*, giving the route additional appeal and popularity. Most climbers are usually torn between the East Face or East Buttress, as both are classic routes. The East Buttress is more sustained and a more direct line, but the East Face has more variety and a richer history. Both routes are about the same level of difficulty.

FA: Robert Underhill, Glen Dawson, Jules Eichorn, Norman Clyde, 8/31.

History

During the 1860s and 1870s there was a certain confusion about which was the Sierra's highest peak. In 1864, Clarence King, while surveying with the California Geological Survey, spied a cluster of high peaks 20 miles distant. In an epic five-day journey with Richard Cotter, he tried to reach the high point already named for Survey leader Josiah Whitney. Standing atop a high peak, the pair were disconcerted to

see the real Whitney several miles away. A second try a few weeks later also failed. Seven years passed before King returned to his nemesis. Clouds obscured the crest during his approach from the east, but soon he stood atop another high peak—surely this was it! He returned satisfied that he had reached his goal. Two years later other explorers discovered that King actually had climbed Mount Langley, a rounded hump five miles south of Whitney and a few hundred feet lower. King entrained from New York when he heard this news, but it was too late: America's true high point had been ascended several times in the preceding month. Francis Fanquhar, the noted Sierra historian, wrote that King was "either a very clumsy mountaineer or a victim of hallucinations."

The 14,496-foot-high mountain soon attracted various agencies and individuals. For a 20-year period the summit area was the most curious military reservation in the land, established for the purpose of conducting high-altitude research into solar radiation. In 1909 a stone hut, which still serves as a summit shelter, was erected by the Smithsonian Institution to protect members who were to determine if Mars had water vapor in its atmosphere. A few years later a biplane flew over the summit, establishing an American altitude record. This event occurred just three days before a significantly more world-shaking one at Sarajevo, which started World War I, and the story of Whitney lay quiescent for more than a decade.

By the late 1920s, the peak had a good trail up its easy side, and the summit was not a lonely place on a summer day. All ascents, except one, had been via the easy south and west flanks. Oddly enough, the exception (which had not been repeated

East Face	Pitch	1	2	3	4	5	6	7	8	9	10	11	12	13
Free difficulty	≥5.10													
	5.9													
	5.8													
	5.7										●			
	5.6	●			●		●	●			●			
	≤5.5		●	●	●		●			●			●	●

for more than half a century) was John Muir's 1873 solo ascent of a steep, narrow couloir just north of the imposing eastern escarpment. Although Muir had warned that "soft, succulent people should go the mule way," his couloir, now known as the Mountaineer's Route, is not difficult and presently is used more often as a descent route than as a way up the peak.

The 2,000-foot-high east face was never considered as a climbing route in the old days, but it definitely attracted attention during 1931, when organized roped climbing made its debut in California. Francis Farquhar had met Robert Underhill in Canada in 1930 and had been impressed with his command of technical climbing. Farquhar cajoled Underhill into visiting California the following year to instruct local climbers on how to use ropes for safety. As recounted earlier, Underhill had enjoyed a productive summer in the Tetons during 1931, and less than two weeks after his bold ascent of the north ridge of the Grand Teton, he was teaching belaying and rappelling to members of a Sierra Club outing in Yosemite. About ten of the most interested climbers migrated south after this introduction, and, with Underhill, made several first ascents in the central Sierra. Whitney's untouched east face was next on their list.

The climbing group had dwindled to five by the time they began the arduous approach to the base of the wall. With Underhill and Farquhar were Jules Eichorn and Glen Dawson, two young men who had never set eyes on the mountain, as well as the already legendary Norman Clyde, a 45-year-old climber who was well known both for his multitude of Sierra first ascents and for the monstrous loads he carried in the high country. Underhill later remarked that Clyde's pack was "an especially picturesque enormity of skyscraper architecture."

It was mid-morning on August 16, 1931, when the five men stood at Iceberg Lake, just below the cliff. The true east face lay to their left; it was so sheer and unbroken that they didn't even consider it. But the right

Chris McNamara

Sarah Felchlin on the airy 5.6 first pitch of the Tower Traverse. Beneath her is 800 feet of air. First Tower is in the background.

side of the face, above the lake, looked more promising. "Suddenly I saw what seemed a just possible route," wrote Underhill in his account of the climb, "and simultaneously Dawson and Eichorn exclaimed to the same effect. It turned out that we all had exactly the same thing in mind. Through the field-glasses we now examined it in detail as well as we could, noting that much of it seemed possible, but that there were several very critical places. Rating our chances of success about 50-50, we were eager to go ahead with the attempt."

Farquhar, out of shape, opted to climb the Mountaineer's Route and meet the victorious climbers on top. The others quickly ascended 600 feet of talus and 3rd class until they reached ledges leading left onto the main face. After a short delay because of routefinding problems, they reached the Washboard, a rippled section of tiered slabs that proved easier than expected. Four hundred feet of 3rd and 4th class rock were rapidly overcome, and the foursome soon reached an exposed wall that offered no immediate way up. The two younger climbers suggested a frontal attack, but, as Underhill put it, "before such a *tour de force* was undertaken Clyde and I urged that a traverse, which we had all already noticed out to the left, be investigated." Clyde later wrote that this traverse "proved to be one requiring considerable steadiness, as the ledges were narrow and there was a thousand feet of fresh air below." The now-famous Fresh-Air Traverse is generally regarded as the crux.

Higher lay the Grand Staircase, a 400-foot section consisting of easy slopes interspersed with short, vertical steps. At the 14,200-foot level, the climbers emerged into an area of excellent, broken rock. Unroping, they wandered individually up the final

few hundred feet, pausing when out of breath to gaze at the astonishingly clear vista. Underhill later wrote that "even the Californians did not succeed in remaining impeccably *blasé*" about the view.

Soon the four climbers were shaking hands with Farquhar. The ascent had taken just three-and-a-quarter hours, a time that is rarely equaled today. While by no means as hard as some of the 1931 Teton routes, it was a memorable ascent and remained the most difficult High Sierra climb throughout the 1930s. Underhill graciously observed that "the beauty of the climb lies chiefly in its unexpected possibility, up the apparent precipice, and in the intimate contact it affords with the features that lend Mount Whitney its real impressiveness."

Eichorn and Dawson soon became leaders in Yosemite Valley rockclimbing, and while they put up many routes more difficult than Whitney, they did not forget their historic climb of the east face. Dawson participated in the second ascent in July 1934, and a month later Eichorn also reascended the wall, inaugurating a variation that has since become the standard first pitch of the route. This variant, known as the Tower Traverse, is located a short distance below the original party's traverse to the Washboard. The Tower Traverse, although short, is terrifically exposed and requires delicate footwork; many climbers consider this 5.6 pitch to be the finest of the route.

Other variations have been made. Two in the vicinity of the Fresh-Air Traverse are named Shaky-Leg Crack (the one considered in 1931 by Eichorn and Dawson) and the Direct Crack, climbed in 1953. Many other routes have been done on the eastern escarpment, and the true east face finally was climbed in 1959.

– Steve Roper

The start of the route. Only the first 60 feet are visible (the Tower Traverse and 5.6 chimney are out of view).

Strategy

Start climbing this route as early as possible. The route only receives direct light from sunrise to about 2 p.m. and can be cold in the shade. Many climbers have underestimated the challenges and length of the climb and had to spend a night (or even two!) on the wall. A 60m rope lets you do the route in a few less pitches, but long pitches will mean poor communication with your belayer.

The start is relatively easy to find: hike up between First and Second Tower and stop before the 800-foot drop off. The first pitch Tower Traverse is one of the most exposed on the route and requires 5.5 face climbing with sparse gear (every 10 feet or so at the crux). The end of the pitch has a short chimney. If wearing a pack, stem as much as possible.

The Fresh-Air Traverse is the routefinding crux of the route. Many people get lost here, usually because they climb up too high. Pause at Belay 6 and study the topo and photo carefully before moving to the alcove belay.

The Fresh-Air Traverse begins with 5.5 moves up and left for 20 feet and then moves horizontally on ledges for 50 feet. Two fixed angle pitons come right before an incredibly exposed move followed by another fixed angle. For the last ten feet you have two options: climb wild and exposed poorly protected 5.6 or stay in the left-facing corner for well-protected but harder moves. If you climb the 5.6 way, try placing gear high in the corner before moving left.

Pitch 8 involves a few chimneys with bad rock. Be careful of loose rock that is often perched right above the belayer.

Pitch 10 is the technical crux of the route and starts with a 5.6 finger crack and ends with difficult 5.7 stemming or offwidth in a corner.

Chris McNamara

After the crux 5.7 corner there are many finishing options. All options will involve about three pitches of mostly 4th- and easy 5th-class climbing and, in general, trend right. The easiest route traverses far right to a small talus field then ascends just left of the ridge.

Retreat

Because the climb traverses, retreat is difficult. Retreat by rappelling the route. One rope works, but two ropes make this easier. You must download Pitches 1, 6, and 7. There are no fixed anchors and a retreat will mean leaving gear. Because most thunderstorms originate from the west, you may not see thunderclouds until they are on top of you.

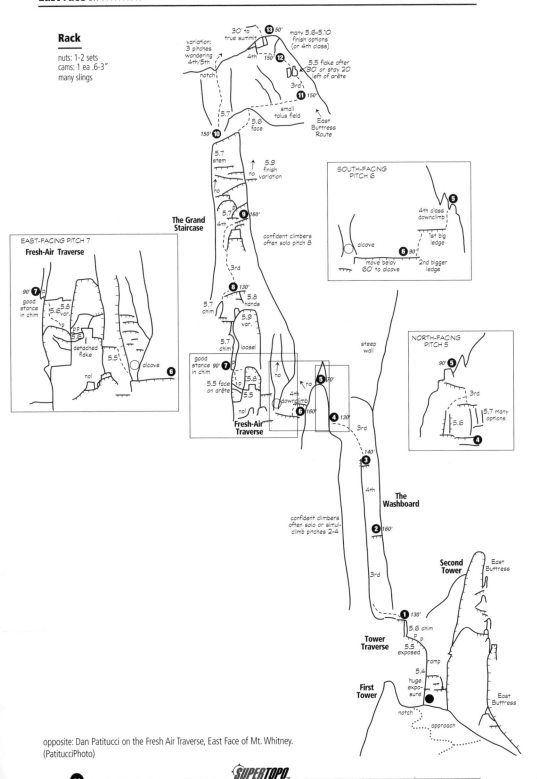

Rack

nuts: 1-2 sets
cams: 1 ea .6-3"
many slings

30' to true summit
13 50'
many 5.6-5.10 finish options (or 4th class)
variation: 3 pitches wandering 4th/5th
4th 150' **12**
5.5 flake after 30' or stay 20' left of arête
notch
3rd
11 150'
5.7
small talus field
East Buttress Route
5.6 face
150' **10**
5.7 stem
5.9 finish variation
no
no
The Grand Staircase
5.7 no
4th **9** 160'
confident climbers often solo pitch 8
3rd
8 130'
5.7 chim
5.8 hands
5.9 var.
5.7 chim
loose!
good stance 90' in chim
7
5.5 face on arête
p
5.8
5.5
no
no
4th downclimb
5 20'
6 160'
Fresh-Air Traverse
4 130'
3rd
3rd
steep wall
140'
3
4th
The Washboard
confident climbers often solo or simul-climb pitches 2-4
2 160'
3rd
Second Tower
East Buttress
1 130'
5.6 chim
p p
Tower Traverse
5.5 exposed
ramp
5.4
huge expo-sure
First Tower
East Buttress
notch
approach

SOUTH-FACING PITCH 6

4th class downclimb
5
1st big ledge
alcove
6 90'
2nd bigger ledge
move belay 60' to alcove

EAST-FACING PITCH 7
Fresh-Air Traverse

90' **7** p
good stance in chim
5.6 var.
5.8
p
p.p 5.6
detached flake
5.5
alcove
no!
6

NORTH-FACING PITCH 5

90' **5**
3rd
5.7 many options
5.6
4

opposite: Dan Patitucci on the Fresh Air Traverse, East Face of Mt. Whitney. (PatitucciPhoto)

East Buttress 5.7★★★★★

Time to climb route:	**4-8 hours**
Approach time:	**3-6 hours**
Descent time:	**3-6 hours**
Sun exposure:	**sunrise to early afternoon**
Height of route:	**1,000'**

The East Buttress may be one of the most classic climbs in the High Sierra. While it does not have the well-known history of the East Face, it is arguably a better route. Unlike the East Face, which makes challenging traverses between long sections of 3rd class, the East Buttress climbs a sustained arête with short and exposed 5.6 or 5.7 sections on almost every pitch.

FA: Bob Brinton, Glen Dawson, Richard Jones, Howard Koster, Muir Dawson, 9/37.

History

Glen Dawson was the finest rock climber in pre-WWII southern California. During the 1930s he used daring skill and occasional piton protection to pioneer the most exciting routes at Tahquitz Rock. On the 1931 first ascent of Mt. Whitney's east face, he, like his ropemates, had been a bit underwhelmed that the imposing face would yield such a modestly challenging route. But he climbed for fun and camaraderie, and in 1934 he came back to make the route's second ascent. At that time he confirmed that the buttress on the right side of the upper face was a proud rib of firm-looking rock, and that it would likely provide a better and more challenging climb with arguably the Sierra's most spectacular position.

During the following two summers Dawson toured and climbed in Europe.

In Germany and Austria he found that climbers were "years ahead of what we were doing in America." He made the hardest climbs of his career there (5.8 or 5.9), and he came back with some advanced skills and an understanding of the German rating system. He introduced this to the Sierra Club, and it evolved into the Class 1-6 system that spread across North America. After his 1936 trip, Dawson returned to Whitney with the now-annual Sierra Club trip. He and Dick Jones got up on that east buttress, but new snow turned them back.

The following Labor Day, Dawson and Jones returned. Teamed with Dawson's brother Muir, Robert Brinton, and Howard Koster, they left camp at Mirror Lake at first light, crossed Pinnacle Ridge, and hiked up to East Face [Iceberg] Lake. From there they scouted the way to climb above the Second Tower toward The Peewee. This was the name Dawson had given to "a hanging rock, which, seen in profile from the trail below Whitney Pass, looks like a huge insect crawling up Mount Whitney."

At the rope-up point, the foot of the Second Tower, they split into two teams. Glen Dawson and Brinton followed Eichorn's Traverse around the left of the tower, while the others circumvented the tower on the right. The teams reunited at the col behind, where Glen Dawson led "directly up a small arête, using two pitons placed the year before." Then Brinton led a pitch keeping to the right of the divide, whereupon Dawson again took the lead up the prow. Glad to have tight-fitting tennis shoes, he made his way "on excellent holds, up the steepest portion of its crest." They continued along the buttress, having to take care where there was fresh snow on ledges. Alongside The Peewee they placed their last of only four pitons on the whole route, and

East Buttress	Pitch	1	2	3	4	5	6	7	8	9	10	11
Free difficulty	≥5.10											
	5.9											
	5.8											
	5.7			●								
	5.6	●	●		●			●	●			
	≤5.5					●	●			●	●	●

soon they were on the summit with plenty of time to hike the trail back to camp. The buttress had proved equal to Dawson's estimation, and he named it the Sunshine Peewee Route, for the perched block and the fact that climbing in the sun was just so much fun.

Two weeks later, Sierra Club members Arthur Johnson and Bill Rice repeated the route, and they needed only the first two pitons. They enjoyed the route so much that they engaged in a fad of the day: they downclimbed the route, and were back at East Face (Iceberg) Lake by 12:30 in the afternoon.

– Andy Selters

Strategy

Start climbing this route as early as possible. The route only receives light from sunrise to about 2 p.m. and can be cold in the shade. A 60m rope lets you do the route in a few less pitches but makes communication with your belayer poor. Every pitch has a great belay ledge.

The start is relatively easy to find: hike to Second Tower and stop at the big left-facing corner. There are two other starting variations to the left that are less direct and not recommended.

Except for the fourth pitch, the first six pitches trend slightly right. For the best climbing, keep to the arête as much as possible. Each pitch has a short, steep, and fun crux followed by 4th class.

From Pitch 7 onward, the route trends left and becomes easier and easier. After Pitch 8, confident climbers often unrope and solo the last three pitches of 4th and easy 5th class. While the summit is often packed with 30+ hikers (and as many cell phones), by stopping just 10 feet below you will not see or hear anyone.

Retreat

Retreat the route by rappelling right (north) into the Mountaineer's Route gully. The higher you climb, the more rappels required. There are no fixed anchors and a retreat will mean leaving gear. Because most thunderstorms originate from the west, you may not see thunderclouds until they are on top of you.

The start of the East Buttress route.

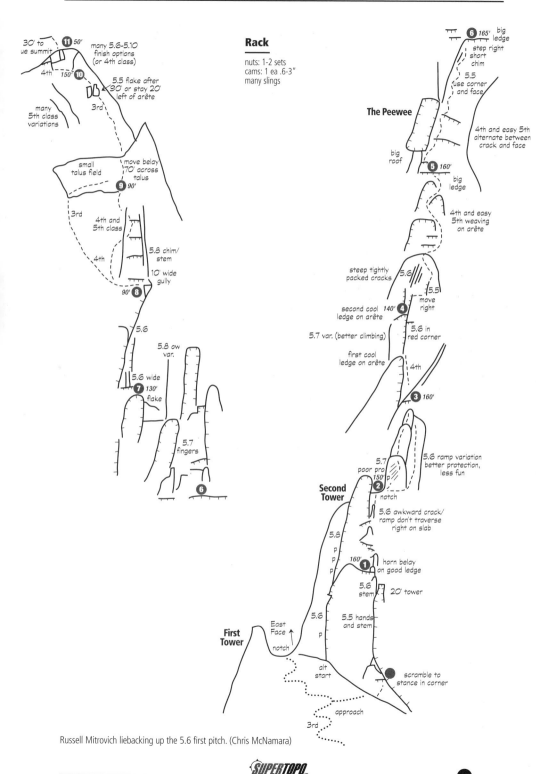

Rack

nuts: 1-2 sets
cams: 1 ea .6-3"
many slings

30' to ue summit **11** 50'
4th 150' **10**
many 5.6-5.10 finish options (or 4th class)
5.5 flake after 90' or stay 20' left of arête
3rd
many 5th class variations
small talus field
move belay 70' across talus **9** 90'
3rd
4th and 5th class
4th
5.8 chim/ stem
10' wide gully **8** 90'
5.6
5.8 ow var.
5.6 wide **7** 130' flake
5.7 fingers
6

6 165' big ledge
step right short chim
5.5 use corner and face
The Peewee
big roof
4th and easy 5th alternate between crack and face
5 160'
big ledge
4th and easy 5th weaving on arête
steep tightly packed cracks 5.6
5.5 move right
second cool 140' ledge on arête **4**
5.6 in red corner
5.7 var. (better climbing)
first cool ledge on arête
4th
3 160'
5.6 ramp variation better protection, less fun
5.7 poor pro 150' p **2**
notch
Second Tower
5.6 awkward crack/ ramp don't traverse right on slab
5.8
p p p 160' **1** horn belay on good ledge
5.6 stem 20' tower
5.6 5.5 hands and stem
First Tower
East Face ↑
notch
p
alt start
scramble to stance in corner
approach
3rd

Russell Mitrovich liebacking up the 5.6 first pitch. (Chris McNamara)

Mountaineer's Route

3rd class★★

Time to climb route: **3 hours**

Approach time: **3-6 hours**

Descent time: **3-6 hours**

Sun exposure: **sunrise to early afternoon**

Height of route: **1,000'**

The Mountaineer's Route is not classic as a climb, but it does offer the most direct non-technical route to the summit of Mt. Whitney. While only rated 3rd class, this is not just a "hike" and many people have died by getting off-route or being under-prepared in spring snow conditions. While technical climbing skills are not needed, routefinding and general "mountain sense" are important.

There are many reasons to climb the Mountaineer's Route. For day hikers, it is a way to avoid the crowds and trail quotas of the Mt. Whitney Trail. For hikers who camp at Iceberg Lake, it is a way to avoid the competitive Mt. Whitney wilderness permit lottery. However, overnight campers still must get a wilderness permit (see "Backcountry Permits" in Introduction, page 24).

FA: John Muir, 10/1873.

Strategy

Some people hike the entire route in a day while most prefer to camp for a night. Start climbing this route as early as possible. The route only receives light from sunrise until about 2 p.m. and can be cold in the shade. The upper gully below the summit is almost always shaded.

The route has two sections. The main lower gully ascends scree (not fun) and a climbers' trail while the last few hundred feet ascend a steep gully on 3rd class and/or snow.

On the lower section, stay on the left side of the gully to avoid scree. Once at the top of the gully, turn 90 degrees left and climb up the first gully you come to. This is the crux. Stay left until the angle steepens and you are forced to the right. One hundred feet of 3rd class scrambling on broken rock leads to the summit.

The route changes dramatically in the winter, spring, and early summer when it is completely covered in snow. When this is the case, many climbers bring crampons, an ice axe, and rope. While the lower gully receives first light and is usually soft, the last 3rd class section rarely receives sun, is icy, and has been the scene of many accidents and deaths. Either come prepared for ice or be ready to climb 4th class and easy 5th class rock to avoid the ice. Most will only want to do the route if it is free of snow, which happens in June or early July, depending on the snow year. Visit the SuperTopo web site to get the latest conditions on the route.

Retreat

To retreat, reverse the route. Be aware that thunderstorms are often unseen until on top of you.

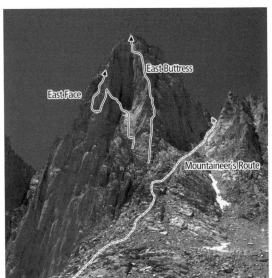

East Buttress

East Face

Mountaineer's Route

Keeler Needle

Keeler Needle's (14,240') massive size and perfect symmetry make it the most striking formation in the High Sierra. In an area packed with inspiring peaks, Keeler stands apart because few ledges interrupt the sheer 1,500-foot face that tapers to a perfect card-table sized alpine summit. If only the rock quality were a little better.

Approach

Follow the Mt. Whitney approach until below the final rock band before Iceberg Lake. The various streams (or trickles) running down this wide rock band are your last sources of water. From here, walk directly to the face over talus to the base of the snowfield.

Descent

From the summit, either head straight for the Whitney summit over talus or walk west until you hit the hikers' trail and follow that up to the summit. Going directly to the summit is faster but more strenuous. From the summit of Mt. Whitney, descend via the Mountaineer's Route.

Chris McNamara

Backcountry Camping

There are two camping options: 1) Upper Boy Scout Lake 2) somewhere between Upper Boy Scout Lake and the base of the climb. Upper Boy Scout has a convenient water source, but you don't get to see the climb. The best option is to camp near the first water source you find once the face of Keeler Needle comes into view.

The view of Pitches 1-7 from on top of the snow field.

Chris McNamara

Harding Route 5.10c★★★

Time to climb route:	**10-14 hours**
Approach time:	**4 hours**
Descent time:	**5 hours**
Sun exposure:	**sunrise to noon**
Height of route:	**1,500'**

At first glance, the Harding Route appears to be the perfect alpine rock climb. Unfortunately, the climbing starts out mildly loose, rotten, and dirty, and mostly stays that way to the summit. We're not talking horrendous and dangerous loose rock, just not the near-perfect Sierra granite on most other routes in this book. That said, climbers still lust after Keeler Needle. It's big, stout, and guarantees a memorable adventure. And, let's face it, it's a big prize that carries a certain amount of bragging rights. This climb is a step up in difficulty from Southwest Face of Mt. Conness.

FA: Warren Harding, Glen Denny, Rob McKnight, Desert Frank, 7/60. FFA: Galen Rowell, Chris Vandiver, Gordon Wiltsie, 8/76.

History

Any peak as spectacular as Keeler Needle is bound to attract the big names in climbing. Warren Harding, the most accomplished big wall first ascensionist in the Sierra Nevada, was joined on the first ascent in 1960 by Glen Denny, Rob McKnight and Desert Frank. The ascent took four-and-a-half days in 1960. Twelve years passed before their route was repeated.

The ascent led to much gossip, especially concerning how Harding coerced Desert Frank to join the expedition. Rumor had it that Frank had never climbed before the ascent and Harding solicited him from a local bar for the sole purpose of carrying the team's wine. Harding staunchly denied these allegations, saying the two actually met in Yosemite's Mountain Room Bar and that he "personally gave Frank quite a few hours of instruction." Harding could never remember Frank's last name, though.

Second Ascent

Throughout the 1960s, lore about Keeler Needle's climbing potential abounded, while the climb repulsed party after party due to the magnitude of the wall and the difficulty of climbing above 14,000 feet elevation.

In March of 1972, Warren Harding, Galen Rowell, and Tim Auger made the second ascent over three days. Their winter ascent was no simple repeat, with Harding dispensing key beta on every pitch. Rowell remembered Harding's especially dim memory, "He answered our questions like a politician answering a query on Vietnam: 'Well, why don't you try it that way and when you get out there if you find that it goes, that's probably it.'" The trio climbed much of the route free, but that didn't make things go necessarily much faster than aid climbing. "…jamcracks at high elevation take almost as long as direct aid," recalled Rowell.

First Free Ascent

In fall of 1976, Rowell returned to Keeler Needle with Chris Vandiver and Gordon Wiltsie to attempt the first free ascent of the route. From his earlier experience on the route, Rowell thought there was a good chance it could go all-free—if a team moved fast and light enough to take advantage of good weather. This would mean eschewing traditional big wall accoutrements such as haul bags, tents, extra fuel and thick, warm sleeping bags.

Harding Route	Pitch	1	2	3	4	5	6	7	8	9	10	11	12	13
Free difficulty	≥5.10		●	●	●			●						●
	5.9	●												
	5.8						●	●		●	●			
	5.7											●		
	5.6													
	≤5.5												●	

The team confronted the first climbing crux less than 200 feet up the 1,800-foot face. A smooth bulge in the rock, broken only by a thin piton crack, thwarted their every move. When an afternoon storm pelted the climbers with rain and snow, they retreated.

Two weeks later they returned and Rowell confidently led this section. The team's conscious decision to move light and fast allowed them to prevail on the pitch. "Most good rockclimbers could have climbed the overhang as I did, without resorting to direct aid… The main reason no one previously free climbed that section of Keeler Needle was that no one had approached the route as an ordinary rockclimb. The east face of Keeler Needle had always been considered a 'big wall,' a multi-day climb requiring direct aid," said Rowell.

There were a couple more dubious sections of climbing on the route. But Vandiver and Rowell spent two days working steadily through each crux. Nearing the summit, Rowell feared a steep aid crack might prove too difficult to free climb. "I did recall a long section of direct aid quite near the top…When we reached the place where I had used direct aid on my winter ascent, we saw an obvious bypass to the difficulties: a system of cracks that in winter had been plastered with snow and unusable…The final pitches went quickly."

First Solo Ascent

In 1986 Walt Shipley made the first free solo ascent of the face. Even under optimal weather conditions, soloing this route is cutting edge. Keeler Needle 5.10c is not like Yosemite 5.10c. It's probably much easier to solo a solid 5.11 like The Rostrum than solo loose 5.10c at 14,000 feet on Keeler. Now take into account that Walt climbed the route in a snow storm. The result was what Peter Croft called in his book *The Good, The Great, And The Awesome,* "one of the most amazing ascents in the area."

– Erik Sloan

Strategy

Only super-fit climbers climb the route car-to-car in a day. Most climbers approach the previous day and camp. You want to be on the climb when the sun hits the wall, just after sunrise. A 60m rope is recommended but not mandatory. Definitely wear a helmet on this climb (it's more for the belayer than the leader).

Many consider the snow field at the base the danger crux of the route. The gullies to the left and right constantly spit rocks so stay away from them. Early in the season, if the snow is soft, kick steps right up the snow. Later in the season, the snow turns to ice and you must bring crampons or climb where the ice meets the rock. Bringing crampons and/or an ice axe is a hassle because you either have to climb with them or toss them back down the snow and retrieve them on the descent. For this reason, most climbers don't bring crampons and just deal.

Once, on the rock, it's a little confusing where to start. In general, stay left when possible for the first few pitches. Pitch 4 is the first offwidth crux. A couple 5-7" cams give added confidence. However, this is the only section of the climb where you need wide gear. As a result, many climbers save weight and leave the wide gear behind and have the offwidth specialist run it out.

Once you reach the first big bivy ledge above Pitch 4, you basically go up and a little right to the steep slightly right-leaning corner out of view to the right. Pitch 7, the Red Dihedral, is the best on the route and involves sustained and overhanging 5.10a hands. There are a few ways to link pitches around here with and without simul-climbing. The strenuous Pitch 8 offwidth crux feels like a couple rounds of sumo wrestling. Fortunately, this section protects with medium cams and a few dicey bolts.

After the offwidth crux comes the routefinding crux. The next two pitches basically wander left a bit, head straight up, and then wander right. There are so many cracks it's hard to draw this on the topo.

Once you reach the big ledge at Pitch 10, you have many options. Right off the ledge, there are numerous delicious stout cracks that most climbers, worn out by now, avoid by escaping right over blocky not-so-classic terrain. Again, it's hard to give beta on this section because the rock is so featured. Traverse way right for an easier escape and worse climbing, or try to get back on the arête/ridge for the best exposure and moves. Either way, you eventually reach the spectacular summit.

One of the main logistical concerns on this climb is how to deal with the pack. You need a fair amount of stuff: approach shoes for the descent, food, water, and some extra warm clothes. However, the steepness of the climb and the offwidth pitches make carrying a pack uncomfortable for the leader and for the follower. Some climbers have the follower carry one big pack and try to haul it over the crux pitches. Other teams have each climber carry small packs, or camelbacks.

Retreat

There are few fixed anchors on this route so any retreat requires leaving gear. Two ropes makes retreat easier but one works. Afternoon thunderstorms are common and the face gets cold when it goes into the shade. Start early and climb fast.

Eric Volz psyching up for the first offwidth crux on Pitch 4.

Chris McNamara

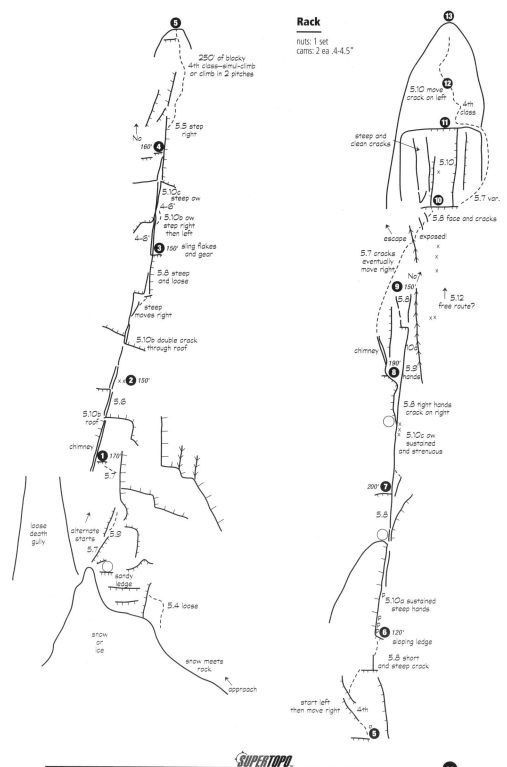

Rack

nuts: 1 set
cams: 2 ea .4-4.5"

250' of blocky
4th class—simul-climb
or climb in 2 pitches

5.5 step
right

No
160'

5.10c
steep ow
4-6"

5.10b ow
step right
then left
4-6"

150' sling flakes
and gear

5.8 steep
and loose

steep
moves right

5.10b double crack
through roof

xx 150'

5.6

5.10b
roof

chimney

170'

5.7

loose
death
gully

alternate
starts

5.9

5.7

sandy
ledge

5.4 loose

snow
or
ice

snow meets
rock

approach

5.10 move
crack on left

4th
class

steep and
clean cracks

5.10
x

5.7 var.

5.8 face and cracks

escape   exposed!
x
5.7 cracks   x
eventually   x
move right,

No
150'

5.8

5.12
free route?

chimney

xx

5.9
hands

190'

5.10d

5.8 tight hands
crack on right

5.10c ow
xx sustained
and strenuous

200'

5.8

5.10a sustained
steep hands

120'
sloping ledge

5.8 short
and steep crack

start left
then move right   4th

Mt. Russell

Mount Russell (14,086')
is the best climbing peak
in the High Sierra for 5.9
and 5.10 climbers. The
routes are long, steep, and
have excellent, golden rock.
Unlike Mt. Whitney, Mt.
Russell has a dramatic
summit (actually, two of
them) with exposure on
all sides. Because of this,
Russell was one of the last
14ers to be climbed in 1926
by Norman Clyde, and you
will rarely see more than a
few other people on the peak.

Russell-Carillon Pass Approach

Approach

For the Fishhook Arête, see the Whitney-
Russell Pass Approach. For the East Ridge,
refer to the Russell-Carillon Pass Approach.

Whitney-Russell Pass Approach
The approach takes most climbers 4 hours
from Whitney Portal, 2 hours from Upper
Boy Scout Lake, and 1 hour from Iceberg
Lake (double times if carrying a heavy
pack). The approach is about 4 miles long
and gains about 5,000 feet in elevation.

Follow the North Fork of Lone Pine
Creek Trail description (see "Mt. Whitney
Approach") to Iceberg Lake. Follow the west
shore of Iceberg Lake and hike northwest
up sandy switchbacks to the notch—this is
the Whitney-Russell Pass. From the notch,
walk north to Mt. Russell up sand, scree,
and talus.

Russell-Carillon Pass Approach
The approach takes most climbers 3.5
hours from Whitney Portal and 1.5 hours
from Upper Boy Scout Lake. The approach
is about 5 miles long and gains about 5,000
feet in elevation.

Follow the North
Fork of Lone Pine Creek
Trail description (see
Mt. Whitney approach
info) until a few
hundred yards east of
Upper Boy Scout Lake
and ascend sandy slopes
to the pass between Mt.
Russell and Mt. Carillon.
When possible, stay
right of sand on rock. It
takes about 1 hour to go
from Upper Boy Scout
Lake to the pass.

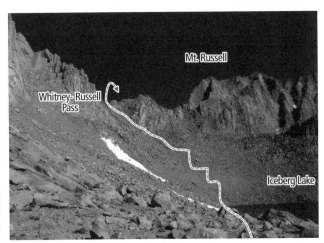

Whitney-Russell Pass Approach

West Summit · East Summit · East Ridge · descent · Fishhook Arête · approach

Chris McNamara

Descent

The descent takes about 2-3 hours from the summit of Mt. Russell to Upper Boy Scout Lake and 1.5 to 2 hours from the summit to Iceberg Lake. There are two recommended options: reverse the East Ridge if you are camped at Upper Boy Scout Lake, or descend the South Face, right side if you are camped at Iceberg Lake.

East Ridge Descent

The East Ridge is one of the best 3rd class routes anywhere so if you are not camped at Iceberg Lake, take this descent. Walk a few hundred yards to the east summit staying just below the ridgeline on the north side. From just below the east summit, move through a notch and downclimb 80 feet of 3rd class and walk over to the East Ridge. Follow the East Ridge down 3rd class occasionally dropping to the north side of the ridge to avoid 4th and 5th class moves. The bottom of the East Ridge ends in the Russell-Carillon Pass. From here walk southeast down scree and sand to Upper Boy Scout Lake.

South Face, Right Side Descent

Pause on the summit to scope it out. A few hundred yards to the east of the west summit (where you are standing) you will see the east summit of Mt. Russell. Between the two summits, an exposed ridge drops down and right and separates two major gullies (you can see the first gully closest to you but not the second). The descent starts on the opposite side of this rock ridge and goes down the second gully. Do NOT take the first gully closest to the west summit!

Walk east on the summit ridge for a few hundred feet until you are about 150 feet from the east summit. Look for 3rd class leading down a chute to a series of ledges in the second (east-most) gully. It is also possible to walk 40 feet past the chute and rappel 140 feet off slung blocks (you may need to provide the slings). Follow a scree trail back to the bottom of Mt. Russell. Reverse the approach.

Backcountry Camping

A few motivated people do the routes car-to-car in a day. Most climbers, however, will want to camp the night before the climb either at Upper Boy Scout Lake if climbing the East Ridge, or Iceberg Lake if climbing Fishhook Arête. Most climbers start hiking early on day one, climb on day two, and descend on day three.

If camping you will need a permit (see "Backcountry Camping Permits" in Introduction).

At both camping areas, the marmots are aggressive and will scarf down all your food if you do not hang it from a boulder or, better yet, bring a bear canister (see "Bears" in Introduction). Also, human waste is a problem in the Whitney area and if you pick up your permit from the Mt. Whitney Ranger Station, you may be required to carry your waste out in a plastic bag.

GPS Coordinates

Approach
For coordinates from the Whitney Portal to Upper Boy Scout Lake, see GPS Coordinates for Mt. Whitney. Also see Mt. Whitney USGS map, page 39.

Between Upper Boy Scout Lake and Russell-Carillon Pass (for East Ridge):
  36° 35' 283", 118° 16' 404"
Russell-Carillon Pass (for East Ridge):
  36° 35' 476", 118° 16' 913"
Russell-Whitney Pass (for Fishhook Arête):
  36° 35' 037", 118° 17' 302"
Start of the Fishhook Arête:
  36° 35' 293", 118° 17' 431"
Russell west summit:
  36° 35' 403", 118° 17' 447"
Russell east summit:
  36° 35' 435", 118° 17' 355"

Chris McNamara

Sarah Felchlin low on Fishhook Arête with Arctic Lakes in the background.

Fishhook Arête 5.9★★★★★

Time to climb route:	**4-7 hours**
Approach time:	**4-7 hours**
Descent time:	**4-7 hours**
Sun exposure:	**late morning to sunset**
Height of route:	**700'**

The Fishhook Arête is one of the more aesthetic arêtes in the High Sierra. Nearly the entire length of the climb is exposed and on perfect golden granite. The climb is easily divided into two distinct arêtes separated by a notch. The lower arête is thin, exhilarating, and diagonals up mostly moderate terrain with a few stout 5.9 sections. The upper arête ascends steep rock that gradually lessens in angle and has incredible belay ledges every 50 feet. While there are only a few brief 5.9 sections, the routefinding difficulties and exposed moves, especially on the first four pitches, make this a climb suitable only for confident 5.9 leaders.

FA: Gary Colliver, John Cleare, 6/74.

Chris McNamara

History

Gary Colliver was a guide and instructor in Yosemite during the early 1970s, and later he became a climbing ranger there. On holidays he often went climbing and cruising through the High Sierra, and in 1971 he was invited to participate in the huge International Himalayan Expedition to the southwest face of Mt. Everest. Although that trip was marketed as a venue for multi-cultural cooperation, it became infamous for eruptive multi-cultural acrimony. One friendship that sprouted, however, was that between Colliver and John Cleare, a British mountaineer and BBC cinematographer.

Soon after that expedition, Cleare got himself a project to tour the world to collect photographs and information that he would compile into the sweeping books, *Mountains* and *The World Guide To Mountains and Mountaineering*. When he got to California in 1974, he naturally hooked up with Colliver. Even though Yosemite climbing was at a peak of intense free-climbing advances, to Cleare an unclimbed route on a wilderness 14er was more interesting. Colliver had planted that seed with a description of Mt. Russell. When they arrived below Russell's broad south face, Colliver pointed out how only two modern ascents had touched the complex peak: Fred Beckey's obscure climb up the north face, and the 5.9 west face that Galen Rowell and Chris Jones had done in 1971. Jones had proclaimed, "the rock is perfect throughout." Thus, the extensive south-facing walls that Colliver and Cleare looked at were a candy shop of untouched terrain.

Colliver let his guest choose their delicacy. "What line shall we try?"

	Pitch							
Fishhook Arête	1	2	3	4	5	6	7	8
Free difficulty	≥5.10							
	5.9	●	●					●
	5.8					●		
	5.7						●	
	5.6							
	≤5.5	●		●	●			

Cleare replied, "Isn't it obvious?" and so they went to the striking staircase-arête that arcs down from the western summit.

Although it was only June, the winter had been a very lean one, and only patches of snow remained. They started right up the first steps of the staircase and followed it as faithfully as possible. A couple pitches up they even straddled its crest, a *chevál*. Colliver was completely in his element as he led up corners and around blocks, slotting occasional hexes and stoppers. Cleare described the climbing as "superb, pitch followed pitch, never hard, never easy, always sustained, interesting, and athletic." But soon Cleare tired, for he was not used to such sustained exertions, much less at gnarly 14,000 feet. Where Colliver danced across face holds and around a dihedral, Cleare looked across with anguish. He struggled to keep his grip, but fell, and fell again. With a rest, he tried again, and "For a split second I hung with my right arm as my feet dropped into space and my left hand slotted in beside the right. I swung my feet onto the tiny nicks on the corner of the dihedral and stepped around onto a small but extremely comfortable ledge."

The skies remained clear, and Colliver finished the leading. Late in the afternoon they made the summit, and Cleare especially enjoyed a panorama sweetened with effort and fatigue. He wrote, "As we ran down the darkening snowfield to Iceberg Lake, we were very happy."

– *Andy Selters*

Strategy

Start early. The route is well-known, but there are rarely more than two parties on the climb at once. A 60m rope will allow you to do the route in one less pitch than listed on the topo. However, long pitches will also mean tough communication, especially on the upper part.

There are many different ways to start the route. Starting outside the arête on the face (the way shown in the topo) is the most challenging, but it is also the easiest to protect and offers the best climbing. If you ignore the topo and start inside the arête you will be faced with about 20 options up different ramps. While a few of these options, if you can find them, may be easier than the 5.9 route shown in the topo, the majority of the options are awkward, difficult to protect, and just not that much fun. A third starting option is to hike up the outside of the arête and do an 80-foot 5.7 pitch to the notch at the base of Pitch 5. This option eliminates most of the routefinding, hard sections, and fun of the route. This is a good option if you get to the base late or are not confident in your routefinding skills on the lower arête.

The third pitch is the routefinding crux of the route. You must move to the left (south) and ascend ramps. Move too far left and you will be lost in a maze of ramps and rope drag. Move too little and the climbing may be steeper and more difficult.

Pitch 4 ends above a notch. The down-climb into the notch is hard, especially with a pack. The first person down sets gear and then belays the second who downleads. Pitch 5 is spectacular and surprisingly easy considering its steepness. Pitch 6 ascends a few wide cracks including a 25-foot-long chimney. Wearing a pack makes this section awkward. Be very careful of pulling on loose blocks in the chimney and, if you want to communicate with your second, set an intermediate belay right at the top of the chimney on a big ledge.

Pitch 7 has at least three variations. Stay mostly on the true arête for the best climbing or move to the right (east) to escape some of the exposure. If you stay mostly on the true arête, after 80 feet, you move left and stem across a wide crack.

Pitch 8 has one short but hard 5.9 off-hands section that will be the crux of the route for people with small hands.

Retreat

For retreat, only one rope is necessary but two ropes make it faster. Between Pitches 1 and 4, rappel on the outside of the arête. Between Pitch 5 and the summit, rappel to the right (east). There are occasionally fixed sling anchors on the arête, but in most retreat scenarios, you will need to leave gear behind. If you see thunderclouds developing to the west, retreat.

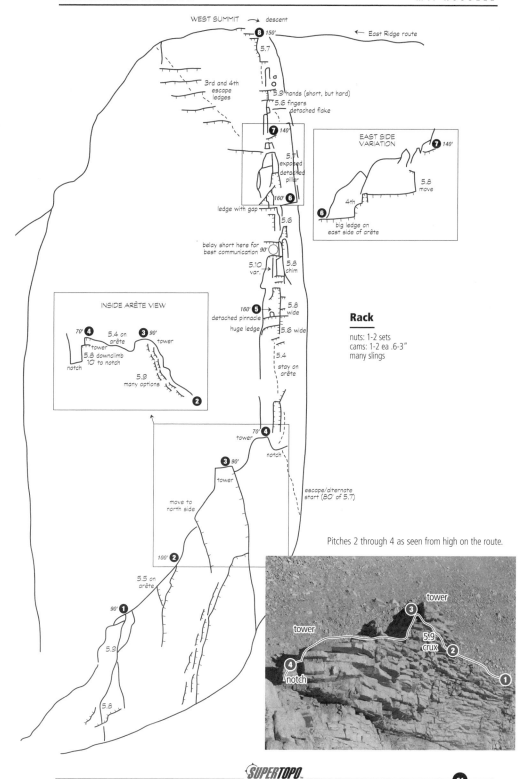

WEST SUMMIT → descent

8 150'   ← East Ridge route

5.7

3rd and 4th
escape
ledges

5.9 hands (short, but hard)
5.6 fingers
detached flake

7 140'

**EAST SIDE
VARIATION**

5.7
exposed
detached
pillar

7 140'

160' **6**

ledge with gap

4th

5.8
move

6

big ledge on
east side of arête

5.6

belay short here for
best communication 90'

5.10
var.

5.8
chim

INSIDE ARÊTE VIEW

160' **5**
detached pinnacle

huge ledge

5.8
wide

5.6 wide

70' **4**   **3** 90'
     5.4 on
tower arête   tower
5.8 downclimb
'10' to notch
notch

5.4
stay on
arête

5.9
many options

2

Rack

nuts: 1-2 sets
cams: 1-2 ea .6-3"
many slings

70' **4**
tower

notch

3 90'

tower

move to
north side

escape/alternate
start (80' of 5.7)

100' **2**

Pitches 2 through 4 as seen from high on the route.

5.5 on
arête

90' **1**

5.9

tower

3

5.9
crux

tower

2

4
notch

1

5.8

East Ridge 3rd class★★★★

Time to climb route: **3-6 hours**

Approach time: **4-7 hours**

Descent time: **4-7 hours**

Sun exposure: **sunrise to afternoon**

Height of route: **800'**

With a striking line, big exposure, and great rock, the East Ridge is one of the best 3rd class routes anywhere. It was by this route that Norman Clyde made the first ascent of Mt. Russell in 1926. While the climb is rated 3rd class, it has a few places where good routefinding skills are critical to avoid climbing harder terrain. In addition, the exposure in some sections makes this much more demanding than the Mountaineer's Route on Mt. Whitney. Overall, this is one of the best 3rd class routes you will ever do.

FA: Norman Clyde, 6/26.

Strategy

Climbing this route is a big day. Start as early as possible so you have plenty of time for the descent. There are rarely crowds.

The crux for many people will be the approach and finding the start of the ridge. Once on the ridge the routefinding is relatively straightforward: stay on the ridge and avoid 4th and 5th class by moving to the right (north) side of the ridge. There are only a few sections where you must move off the main ridge. The first one comes about halfway up the ridge and the second just below the east summit. These sections are above slabs that drop away to vertical face and may be unnerving for hikers unaccustomed to exposure.

During the early season there may be snow on the north side of the ridge that will force you to take a more direct line on the ridge. In this case, you may have to climb 4th or 5th class terrain.

Retreat

Retreat at any time by reversing the route.

above: Mt. Russell's East Ridge from the summit of Mt. Whitney.
opposite: The West and South Faces of Mt. Russell seen at sunset from the Summit of Mt. Whitney. (Chris McNamara)

Chris McNamara

Charlotte Dome

Squarely in the middle of the Sierra Nevada sits Charlotte Dome (10,690'), home to what Todd Vogel feels is the best rock climb of its grade in the range, probably in California, and perhaps the West. The monstrous 1,200-foot-tall dome is one of those compelling formations that begs to be climbed. The setting for this climb is what makes it a classic instead of merely a great climb. Situated near the head of Kings Canyon, the hike in is spectacular, and the views from the climb are outrageous. It is no surprise then that this climb is included in Roper and Steck's *Fifty Classic Climbs of North America*.

Approach

There are two approaches: from the east side of the Sierra out of Onion Valley, or from the west side of the Sierra out of Kings Canyon National Park. The western approach is slightly shorter than the eastern approach but involves much more elevation gain (from the west you start at 5,000 feet and from the east you start at 9,200 feet). Also, on the eastern approach, the campsite is much closer to the start of the climb, making for an easier climbing day. From the west, you must climb 2,000 feet on unenjoyable terrain from your campsite to the start of the climb—a rough way to start the morning. The downside of approaching from the east is that you never get a good look at the climbing route. From either side, most parties use a full day for the approach, a full day on the route, and a full day to return to the trailhead.

Western Approach from Kings Canyon National Park

From Fresno, take Highway 180 to Kings Canyon National Park. Drive through Cedar Grove to Road's End.

The approach takes most climbers 4-6 hours from Road's End (the end of Highway 180) to the camping at Charlotte Creek (gaining 2,300 feet in elevation) and another 2 hours from there to the base of the climb (gaining 2,100 feet in elevation). The entire approach involves about 7 miles of travel on trail, 1.5 miles on climbers' trail, and gains a total of about 4,400 feet in elevation. Temperatures on the approach are scorching in the summer so you should start hiking at dawn.

South Face

Karl Lew

From Road's End, hike east on the Woods Creek Trail for 2 miles and turn right onto the Bubbs Creek Trail. Hike 5 miles to the junction of Bubbs Creek and Charlotte Creek, which is the camping spot. This first section consistently and gently climbs uphill except for the initial steep switchbacks getting into the Bubbs Creek drainage. The second part of the approach is anything but gentle.

From the camping spot at the junction of Bubbs Creek and Charlotte Creek, follow a climbers' trail on the east side of Charlotte Creek. This section is steep, grueling, and will probably involve some unpleasant bushwhacking (bring long pants). Stay along Charlotte Creek, occasionally navigating some rock, until it is easy to traverse left on slabs to the base. Do not traverse too early or you may need to climb extra slab pitches to reach the base.

Eastern Approach from Onion Valley

Take U.S. 395 to Independence (45 minutes south of Bishop, 15 minutes north of Lone Pine). Last minute supplies can be found here, but if you need anything more than basic food, go to Bishop. From the center of town, drive west on the Onion Valley Road for 20 minutes (14 miles) to Onion Valley trailhead at the end of the road.

The approach takes most climbers 5-7 hours from the trailhead to the best camping spot and another 45 minutes to the base of the climb. The approach involves about 8 miles of travel on trail and 4 miles of climbers' trail and cross-country travel. You gain about 2,500 feet to get over Kearsarge Pass and lose about that much before reaching the base of the climb. This means the hike out is about as difficult as the hike in.

From Onion Valley, hike the Kearsarge Pass Trail for 4 miles to Kearsarge Pass (11,811 feet). From here, the summit of Charlotte Dome is barely visible down the valley to the west. A steep 0.25-mile descent leads to a fork in the trail. Stay on the right (north) fork (do not go down to Bullfrog Lakes) and continue another 2 miles to the intersection with the Muir Trail and take the left fork. You're only on the Muir Trail

for a few minutes before leaving it to head west to Charlotte Lake.

Here the approach gets interesting. Go 200 yards past the lake and cross its outlet on the well-defined trail and continue downstream. This is the start of the old Gardiner Pass Trail. It crosses a talus slope, an open meadow, and heads back into forest where it passes through a packers' drift fence (close the rails if you find them closed).

After crossing to the north side of Charlotte Creek the trail is good for 0.25 mile and then it becomes indistinct amidst small trees and downed dead trunks. Watch for cairns for 0.5 mile until the trail becomes well-defined again. Cross a stream (10,070 feet) amidst forest and continue through the trees until they open out onto a dry, open manzanita and grass slope. Continue over this and cross a stream in an open gully (9,890 feet). Looking west toward Charlotte Dome, you should be able to see a large forested bench east of the dome, at and slightly above your elevation. This is your camp destination. The trail enters the forest again and passes through an area of aspen and pine. Emerge onto a second manzanita slope and drop down the sandy trail 500 yards to 9,740 feet. At this point, the trail to the base continues on down the canyon. If you are not camping, take this trail and it will get you directly to the base of the climb.

If camping however, look for a large rock cairn and a poor trail that leads upward across the open slope. Follow cairns across to an open gully with some rock slabs. Pass below the slabs and look for cairns. Sometimes you'll have a great series to follow and good trail, other times it will disappear for hundreds of feet. It is never necessary to drop below 9,800 feet. Once back in the forest, the trail is well-cairned. Keep heading toward the ridge that runs off the north side of Charlotte Dome, and cross some moraine ridges before running up against this ridge. Look for a great campsite (10,140 feet) on the east side of the creek adjacent to a lush spring right where the old trail heads up to Gardiner Pass. This site is little used and beautiful. Please take care to leave it this way.

To approach the climb, follow the west side of the creek, head through the woods trending right and leave the forest and come out onto slabs. Continue to descend until you can see the tops of some trees across the slabs toward the start of the climb. Follow the best and easiest line across to these trees. Follow cairns and a poor trail through manzanita and across slabs toward the lowest point of the south face. Total descent from camp is about 730 feet.

Descent

Scramble due north on 3rd class until you can gain the easy slabs that head back to the east. If you camped on the 10,300-foot plateau, you've got about 45 minutes of descending from the summit. If you're down in Bubbs Creek, take a handful of ibuprofen and keep heading down that hill.

Backcountry Camping

The best camping spot on the western approach is at the junction of Bubbs Creek and Charlotte Creek. This is a popular spot and has a bear box for your food, which may be full with other campers' food. Another strategy would be to camp at the base of the route where there are small open camp spots (bivies, really). However, Charlotte Creek, the water source, is a good walk away so plan on bringing a water bag if this is your strategy. You can also camp at small sloping sites on Charlotte Creek and have a shorter but still unpleasant manzanita bash to the start of the route.

The best camping spot from the east side is the spot at 10,140 feet described in the Eastern Approach from Independence/ Onion Valley. Another option is to camp at Charlotte Lake, but this will commit you to a much longer climbing day.

You will need a wilderness permit to camp (see "Backcountry Camping Permits" in the Introduction, page 24).

South Face

descent

camping

Todd Vogel

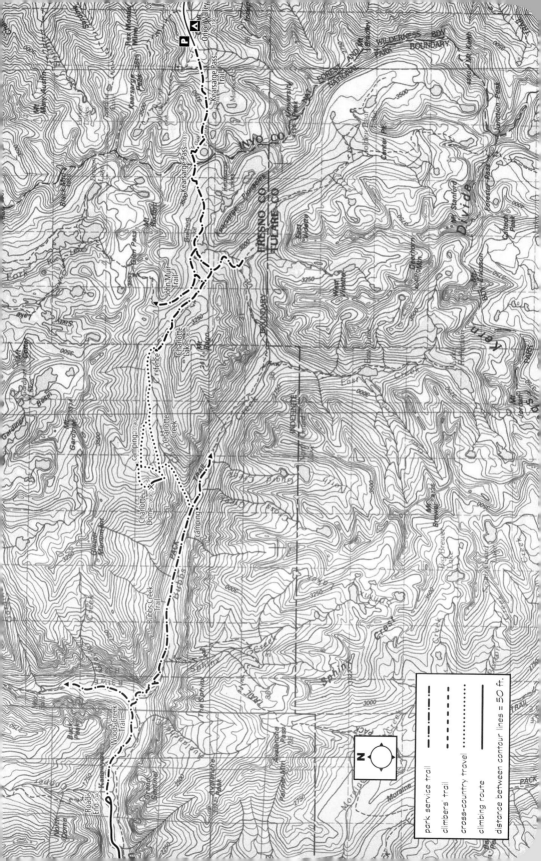

South Face 5.8★★★★★

Time to climb route: **5-9 hours**

Approach time: **6-9 hours**

Descent time: **6-9 hours**

Sun exposure: **all day**

Height of route: **1,200′**

The South Face of Charlotte Dome has hundreds of different variations. We have provided a topo of the easiest way to climb the face. However, because it is easy to get off-route, you should be confident leading 5.9 before climbing this route. You should also be confident placing gear on discontinuous and devious cracks. The rock and the climbing are reminiscent of Tuolumne Meadows: long, smooth faces that appear to be impossible from a distance are actually covered with knobs and texture, allowing for relatively easy climbing. Many water grooves and solution pockets make the climbing additionally manageable and totally unique—how often do you get to climb "furrows"?

FA: Galen Rowell, Chris Jones, Fred Beckey, 10/70.

History

It is unusual in North American climbing history for the first ascent of a climb of this quality to come as late as 1970, especially since Charlotte Dome was one of the first monoliths noted in the High Sierra. During the summer of 1864, members of the California Geological Survey camped just below the dome at Charlotte Creek. Charles Hoffmann sketched the peak, and William Brewer, the field leader of the survey, described it in his journal as "a grand smooth granite rock."

Generations of John Muir Trail backpackers have seen the dome from the Glen Pass region, some 20 miles north of the Mt. Whitney massif. Among these walkers must have been hundreds of rockclimbers who surely commented upon the formation only 2 miles distant. Yet for some reason Peak 10,690 remained for decades just a designation on the map rather than an entry in a climbing guide. Perhaps the idea of carrying a pack full of iron for ten miles—the nearest road is that far—discouraged would-be pioneers. After all, closer chunks of granite beckoned.

When Chris Jones, Fred Beckey, and Galen Rowell approached Charlotte Dome in October 1970, they carried heavy packs indeed, for a previous long-distance reconnaissance had indicated a long, steep, and blank wall. With only a weekend at their disposal, it was obvious to the trio that they would have to make a one-day effort or none at all. With the short autumn days, this limitation posed a potential problem. When the climbers arrived under the face, they blanched, for there were absolutely no continuous crack systems, and the wall approached verticality in several places. Bolt ladders might be necessary, they thought, and the climb could take several days. To the side of the south face, however, the cliff looked more feasible, and Beckey insisted that this was the logical way to go. Reluctantly, the other two agreed.

When the three men actually set foot on the rock, they were pleasantly surprised, for the golden granite bristled with flakes and "chickenheads," the doorknob-like protrusions that occur on certain types of weathered granite. Although Beckey remained committed to his proposed route, Rowell and Jones thought they could piece together a direct line up the south face, hoping that blank-appearing walls would yield knobs. Jones later wrote that they felt it was "better to retreat off a good climb

South Face	Pitch	1	2	3	4	5	6	7	8	9	10	11	12
Free difficulty	≥5.10												
	5.9												
	5.8						•		•				
	5.7				•		•	•		• •		•	
	5.6	•											
	≤5.5		•	•							•		

than to succeed on an indifferent one." With this noble attitude, the threesome roped up.

After a few easy pitches on the apron at the base of the face, the climbers encountered the first problematical section, a steep headwall capped with a short vertical step. The first part of this obstacle was overcome by means of copious hidden holds. And just when these vanished, cracks appeared, and a few 5.7 moves led through the impressive step. By the time the pioneers had gathered atop this pitch, they realized that they had discovered a real gem of a climb. But with three climbers the going was slow, and the sun already was at its zenith. Beckey, still unhappy about the rash decision to push for a direct route, volunteered to jumar up a fixed rope, thus freeing the second man to belay the leader. Self-belayed, Beckey could proceed at his own pace. The climbers thought this clever idea might just get them back to warm sleeping bags that night.

Several pitches higher the incredulous climbers, almost sated with chickenheads, came up against a fabulous wall known now as the Furrow Pitch. This steep, 100-foot section dominates the central part of the route and hovers ominously over the lower-angled slabs below. Great grooved ruts, some of them three feet deep, scar the otherwise monolithic granite, as if some gigantic feline had sharpened its claws there during primordial times. The Furrow Pitch is not difficult—the only real problem is choosing the easiest slit—but it is the most memorable of many sterling pitches.

An enormous ledge not far above this pitch proved perfect for a brief lunch stop, brief because the sun was sinking disturbingly low in the west. Several more pitches, liberally sprinkled with knobs, went quickly, and soon Rowell's shouts told the others he was on top. The splendid summit boulders were still aglow when Jones and Beckey arrived, though Charlotte Creek

The wildly featured rock on Pitches 2 through 5.

already was cloaked in shadow. Fortunately, the descent proved easy and rapid, and the pessimistic Beckey was amazed as they strutted into camp before pitch dark.

– Steve Roper

Strategy

With a summit elevation of "only" 10,690 feet, Charlotte Dome has a longer climbing season than most Sierra climbs. Even after the first few big snowstorms of the fall it is generally possible to have good climbing conditions. The route faces south and dries quickly, and mid-winter ascents using skis to approach and return, though rare, are not unheard of.

This is a big and popular climb so get a dawn start. If starting from the junction of Charlotte Creek and Bubbs Creek, get a predawn start.

The route has a reputation for difficult routefinding, but if you can find the start you'll probably do okay on the route. The climb begins just west of the lowest point on the center of the south face. There's a large amphitheater to the left and a small depression to the right. Scramble over a 4-foot diameter fallen dead tree 100 feet below the start. Three or four live pines are climber's left of the actual start. Also look for a double forked tree near the start. Start by climbing a 30-foot-tall, 4-foot-deep left-facing corner that lead to an 8-inch diameter pine at the end of the first pitch.

The crux sixth pitch, "The Slot" follows hand crack through a steep area to a small stance atop a dike.

Pitch 8 offers interesting 5.8 face and crack climbing in a chimney-type feature. The exposure is tremendous with thousands of feet of air down to Bubbs Creek.

Above, the routefinding is a bit of a Zen affair where just about everything is climbable. The best line goes pretty much straight up, with rare detours to place protection (bizarre and questionable nut and cam placements; knob tie-off), to a sloping ledge. If the common mid-day winds kick up, get ready for some excitement.

The hard stuff is behind you now, but you still have four pitches to go, the first of which is the famous Furrows Pitch. Head up and left to the cool and easier-than-it-looks prow, which is grooved by the giant furrows. These are deep erosional features with sharp edged fins and deep pockets between them.

Retreat

Retreat by rappelling the route with two 50m or 60m ropes (with only one rope you will have to leave a ton of gear). There are usually fixed rap anchors on the first five pitches. Above here, you will have to leave your own gear.

Todd Vogel

Climbing "The Slot" Pitch 6.

page 72: David Melkonian in front of Temple Crag. (PatitucciPhoto)

Rack

nuts: 1-2 sets
cams: 1-2 ea .6-3.5"
many slings

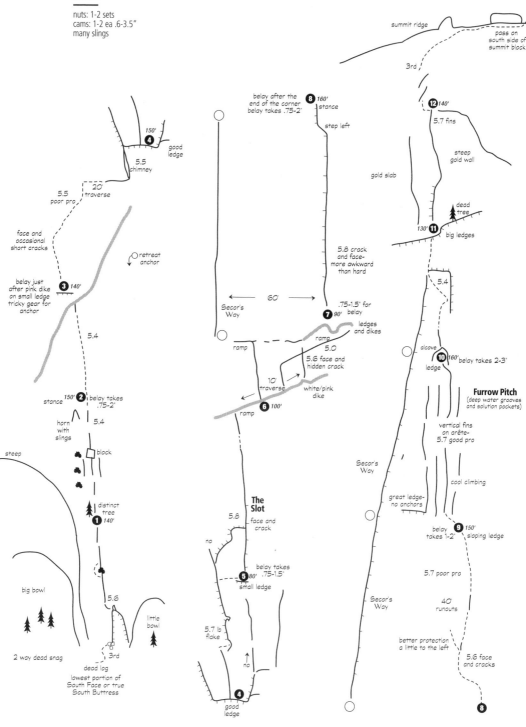

summit ridge

pass on south side of summit block

3rd

12 140'

5.7 fins

steep gold wall

gold slab

dead tree

11 130' big ledges

5.4

belay after the end of the corner belay takes .75-2"

8 160' stance

step left

5.8 crack and face-more awkward than hard

.75-1.5' for belay

7 90'

ledges and dikes

ramp

5.0

5.6 face and hidden crack

white/pink dike

alcove

10 160' belay takes 2-3'
ledge

Furrow Pitch
(deep water grooves and solution pockets)

vertical fins on arête-5.7 good pro

cool climbing

4 150'
good ledge

5.5 chimney

5.5 poor pro

20' traverse

retreat anchor

face and occasional short cracks

belay just after pink dike on small ledge tricky gear for anchor

3 140'

5.4

Secor's Way

60'

ramp

10' traverse

ramp

6 100'

great ledge-no anchors

belay takes 1-2'

9 150' sloping ledge

5.7 poor pro

40' runouts

Secor's Way

stance 150' **2** belay takes .75-2"

horn with slings

5.4

steep

block

big bowl

2 way dead snag

distinct tree

1 140'

5.6

little bowl

3rd

dead log

lowest portion of South Face or true South Buttress

The Slot

5.8 face and crack

no

belay takes .75-1.5'

5 80'
small ledge

5.7 lb flake

no

no

4
good ledge

Secor's Way

Secor's Way

better protection a little to the left

5.6 face and cracks

8

Temple Crag

Temple Crag (12,999') is one of the most massive chunks of rock in the High Sierra. The 0.5-mile-wide and 2,200-foot-tall dark, ominous-looking rock is carved into a series of large gullies and striking arêtes. The three most prominent arêtes—Sun Ribbon Arête, Moon Goddess Arête, and Venusian Blind—are collectively known as the Celestial Arêtes. They all have similar character—long, exposed, and incredibly fun. The rock, which from a distance looks like choss, is mostly solid and has an authentic alpine feel. Whether you climb 5.7 or 5.12, all Temple Crag routes are packed with adventure.

Approach

From U.S. 395 in the middle of Big Pine, take the Glacier Lodge Road for 20 minutes (14 miles) almost to its end. Park at the hiker parking area at the trailhead for the North Fork of Big Pine Creek Trail.

The approach takes around 4 hours from the parking area to the base of the climb (double times if carrying a heavy pack) and involves 5.5 miles on the main trail, one mile on climbers' trail, 0.5 mile of cross-country travel, and gains about 3,500 feet in elevation.

From the hikers' parking area, follow the North Fork of Big Pine Creek Trail for 5.5 miles to Third Lake. Pause here (or at Second Lake) to identify your route. As with all Sierra climbs, the route line is less obvious once you get up close.

Approach from Third Lake

Leave the trail and walk cross-country to the outlet at the east end of Third Lake (last water in late season). Cross the creek and follow a climbers' trail up and right for a few hundred feet to a talus field. Cross the talus field and locate a faint climbers' trail that follows the edge of where the light and dark talus/scree meet. Follow this until you are almost under the snow gully to the right of Moon Goddess Arête. Delay hiking up the steep scree to the base as long as possible. It takes about an hour to get from Third Lake to the start of the route.

All routes start with a snow field. In warm weather, avoid the need for crampons by hiking up to the snow fields the afternoon before your climb and punching in "stairs" while the snow is soft. Expect firm snow the next morning (ice axe recommended), but if you did a good job with your steps, crampons are unnecessary. Another option for Moon Goddess Arête and Venusian Blind is to climb the 5.6 chimney variation to the first pitch that is shown in the topos.

SP Parker

Approach from Second Lake

This is a more direct approach involving trickier routefinding than the Third Lake approach, but may be easier in periods of high runoff since it avoids the creek crossing. Leave the main trail at Second Lake (last water in late season) and follow the south side of the lake first on a trail then on talus to the base of a sandy moraine. Here you'll find faint trails ascending the sand and scree of the moraine (this is the moraine that descends from Contact Pass). If heading just to the base to climb, as opposed to heading to find a camp, you'll follow these faint trails all the way up the moraine toward the climbs.

Descent

The descent takes 1-2 hours from the summit of Temple Crag back to Second Lake or Third Lake. From the summit, hike east down a disjointed climbers' trail directly toward Contact Pass. Don't get suckered down a gully leading right (south). The trail eventually becomes 3rd class and then, 100 feet before Contact Pass, turns to steep 4th and 5th class. Most climbers make an 80-foot rappel from slings down this last section instead of downclimbing. From the base of the rappel at the highest point of Contact Pass, follow the climbers'

trail north down sandy switchbacks into talus. Here it is crucial to stay right (away from Temple Crag) or you will either a) end up in a dangerous snow gully or b) end up on a loose and dangerous sandy slope. (However, in early season, if the snow gully is soft enough, it can offer the fastest way down.) The talus ends once you are even with the start of the route. From here, walk out the way you came in to Second Lake or Third Lake.

Backcountry Camping

Good sites are located near the outlets of Second Lake (less crowded) and Third Lake (more crowded). Both lakes have an emerald green color (due to glacial silt) and a clear view of all Temple Crag routes.

In addition, there are nice spots located immediately below the Dark Star Buttress of Temple Crag. These spots are close to the climbs and away from the main trail. In later season, these spots usually require a 10-minute walk for water to the inlet of Third Lake. These sites necessitate carrying your overnight pack over the small moraines that project from the crag toward Third and Second Lake, an arduous task.

You will need an overnight permit. (See "Backcountry Camping Permits" in the Introduction, page 24.)

Matt White

Venusian Blind 5.7★★★★★

Time to climb route:	**4-8 hours**
Approach time:	**4 hours**
Descent time:	**5 hours**
Sun exposure:	**morning to afternoon**
Height of route:	**1,500'**

Venusian Blind ascends one of the many striking arêtes on Temple Crag. The route is packed with fun climbing and wild exposure. It is shorter than Moon Goddess Arête, more continuous, and arguably better. It's a little longer than the East Buttress of Whitney and some consider it more classic.

FA: Don Jensen, S. Petroff, A. Walker, 8/69.

History

On August 12, 1969, Don Jensen went with clients up on his third Celestial Arête in three weeks; this time it was the shorter and easier one near Temple Crag's eastern edge. He would name it the Venusian Blind, for the sight of Venus rising behind it at dawn. Leading S. Petroff and A. Walker, he worked from "the flatiron" up through the complex but not difficult towers above, rating one pitch 5.6. Unlike the longer arêtes he'd started to the right, he was able to complete this one on the first attempt. He described the route as "an excellent beginner's climb in the range. Moderate difficulty occurs throughout the climb, but the difficulties are short and not very exposed."

– Andy Selters

Strategy

All but the fastest teams should hike in and camp the day before the climb (see Camping). If climbing the route car-to-car in a day, get a predawn start. This route can be popular at times, but there are many ways to pass parties.

The start is not totally obvious as you must cross a vast expanse of 3rd class where there are many options. After Pitch 1, at the point where the 4th class turns briefly back into 3rd class, you'll trend up and left for another 300 feet, heading for a series of 40- to 60-foot-tall right-facing corners. The route starts at the highest of these, on the left side of a feature that is more a blunt buttress than an arête. There is a minor true arête to the right of this feature that joins the buttress several hundred feet higher. It works to climb this, too, but it is quite loose and not recommended.

The routefinding difficulties come on Pitch 5. Move left across a small gully onto the right side of an emerging sharp arête. Here there are two options: climb directly up the right side of the face, angling slightly left, or move left, working around a small roof, through a steep area, and back right to join the first option. While both ways are slightly runout, the left option has better climbing and more solid rock.

For the next several pitches, follow the topo closely.

The last four pitches are challenging to protect, especially from the second's perspective so if you're with someone less experienced you should opt for the rappel below Pitch 10.

Once on the summit plateau, continue for 20 minutes on 3rd and 4th class to the summit.

Retreat

It is possible to retreat using one 50m or 60m rope. Generally, escape is made to the right. It is not as easy to escape Venusian Blind as it is Moon Goddess Arête; for this reason if the weather is questionable or other factors exist, Moon Goddess Arête may be a better choice.

Venusian Blind	Pitch	1	2	3	4	5	6	7	8	9	10	11	12
Free difficulty	≥5.10												
	5.9												
	5.8												
	5.7			●		●			●	●			
	5.6							●					
	≤5.5	●	●	●		●		●				●	●

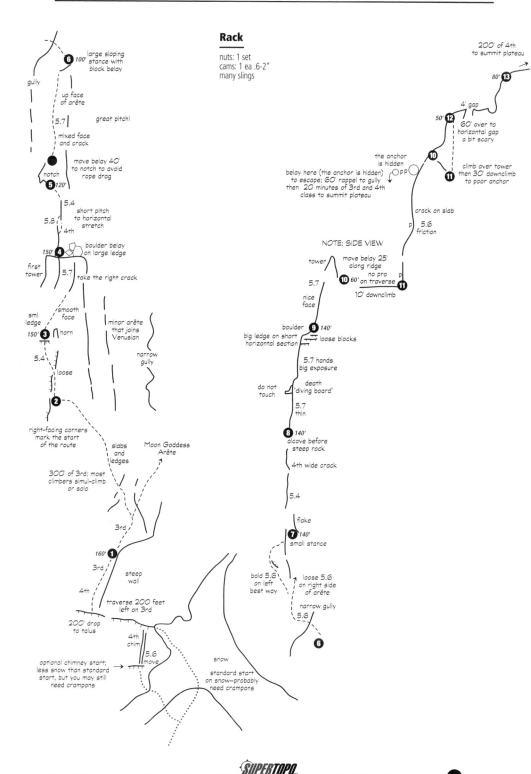

Rack

nuts: 1 set
cams: 1 ea .6-2"
many slings

6 100' large sloping stance with block belay

gully

up face of arête

5.7   great pitch!

mixed face and crack

move belay 40' to notch to avoid rope drag

notch

5 120'

5.4   short pitch to horizontal stretch

5.8

4th

boulder belay on large ledge

150' **4**

first tower

5.7   take the right crack

sml ledge   smooth face

150' **3**   horn

5.4   minor arête that joins Venusian

loose

narrow gully

2

right-facing corners mark the start of the route

slabs and ledges

Moon Goddess Arête

300' of 3rd: most climbers simul-climb or solo

3rd

160' **1**

3rd

steep wall

4th

traverse 200 feet left on 3rd

200' drop to talus

4th chim

5.6 move

snow

optional chimney start; less snow than standard start, but you may still need crampons

standard start on snow—probably need crampons

200' of 4th to summit plateau

80' **13**

4' gap

50' **12**

60' over to horizontal gap a bit scary

the anchor is hidden

10

belay here (the anchor is hidden) to escape; 60' rappel to gully then 20 minutes of 3rd and 4th class to summit plateau

OPP

11

climb over tower then 30' downclimb to poor anchor

crack on slab

p   5.6 friction

NOTE: SIDE VIEW

tower

move belay 25' along ridge

5.7   no pro
10 60' on traverse

10' downclimb

11 p

nice face

boulder **9** 140'

big ledge on short horizontal section   loose blocks

5.7 hands big exposure

do not touch   death "diving board"

5.7 thin

8 140'
alcove before steep rock

4th wide crack

5.4

flake

7 140'
small stance

bold 5.6 on left best way

loose 5.6 on right side of arête

narrow gully

5.6

6

Moon Goddess Arête

5.8★★★★

Time to climb route: **6-10 hours**

Approach time: **4 hours**

Descent time: **5 hours**

Sun exposure: **morning to afternoon**

Height of route: **1500'**

There are few 5.8 routes in the High Sierra with more continuous exposure. The climbing is moderate but wild and follows a striking arête from start to finish. While the climb ascends many sections of detached blocks, few areas are dangerously loose. This route has a reputation of being big, committing, and one of the finest 5.8 climbs in the High Sierra.

FA: Don Jensen, J. Conners (lower part), 1969.
Carl Dreisbach, Pat Armstrong (entire route), 1969.

History

On August 5, 1969, a week after Don Jensen had taken two clients up on the Sun Ribbon Arête, he led another client onto the arête to the left, which he would call the Moon Goddess Arête. Again he was thrilled to find firm rock and enjoyable, moderate climbing. At the first major gendarme, he placed a piton and led around its right side to the notch behind, and then did another pitch (which he rated 5.4) halfway up the adjoining tower. A cautious man, Jensen from there chose to escape into the 3rd/4th class gully to the left, and continue to the top that way.

On September 2 that same summer, Carl Dreisbach and Pat Armstrong decided

to finish the Moon Goddess. On the same day, Jensen and John Fischer would climb the complete Sun Ribbon. They would culminate the Summer of Celestial Arêtes with simultaneous ascents. Dreisbach and Armstrong followed Jensen's earlier path up the Moon Goddess, and at the major tower they worked right across steep and exposed terrain to cracks that led to the top of the tower. Whooping back and forth across a profound chute with Jensen and Fischer, Dreisbach and Armstrong followed their arête to the upper slopes of Temple Crag.

– Andy Selters

Strategy

Get a dawn start or, if climbing the route car-to-car in a day, get a predawn start. This route can be popular at times, but luckily there are many ways to pass parties.

The first half of the climb ascends a broad arête of mostly 4th class with the occasional 5.6 move. This arête is much longer than it appears from the base. For the best rock and best climbing, stay on the true arête as much as possible. On this section, as for most of the climbs, there are many good ledges or stances to belay from. As is shown by the general nature of the topo, there are no defined or "correct" belay stances. Climb until you run out of rope and belay.

Pitch 6, the First Tower has the wildest climbing on the route. Don't be tempted to run this pitch all the way to the notch or heinous leader-paralyzing rope drag will result. Instead, the leader should trend high when rounding the steep face, aiming for a small horn/tower above the notch and belay there. Have the second stay low, below

Moon Goddess Arête	Pitch	1	2	3	4	5	6	7	8	9	10	11	12	13	14
Free difficulty	≥5.10														
	5.9														
	5.8							●	●						
	5.7					●							●		
	5.6						●			●				●	
	≤5.5	●	●	●	●	●			●		●				

your stance, and belay them directly to the notch. Rap or downclimb off the horn.

Note: For the short version of Moon Goddess Arête, continue up the chimney above, exiting to the left at the top of the chimney. A short rap leads into the gully, but instead of escaping down the gully, four pitches of 4th class leads to the summit plateau. Done this way, Moon Goddess Arête is mostly 4th class with only 10 feet of 5.7.

From the large ledge above the notch, climb the chimney then exit right to a 20-foot-long left-facing corner (5.8). With the massive Ibrium Tower above, wander up the face for 100 feet to a nice ledge on the right edge where the northwest face and northeast face meet. Here, the route leaves the arête on a two-pitch traverse around Ibrium Tower.

Pitch 10 is often missed by climbing too high on 5.8 terrain (many bail slings are visible). Be sure to start by downclimbing 10 feet to a sloping but easy ledge system that traverses 140 feet horizontally across the face. If you are making 5th class moves on the traverse, you are too high. Follow the ledge to the base of a 20-foot-wide gully that leads straight up. From the top of the gully, 140 feet of sometimes-loose 5.7 regains the arête/ridge. From here, several short pitches, downclimbing, and a rappel lead to the open scree and talus field of the summit plateau. Continue for 20 minutes on 2nd/3rd class to the summit. The incredible Palisades view and big exposure on the summit "island" are not to be missed.

The second pitch and above as seen from Belay 1 at the top of the 4th class.

Retreat

It is possible to retreat using one 50m or 60m rope. Retreat from First Tower or below by rappelling into the gully that is climber's left of the arête. The next easy place to retreat comes on Pitch 12 where it is again possible to rappel into the gully on the climber's left. However, by this point, it is much easier to climb two more easy pitches and join the ridge. For all other pitches between 7 and 12, you may need to rappel/reverse the route before it is possible to enter the escape gully.

Rack

nuts: 2 sets
cams: 1 ea .6-2"
many slings

SOUTHEAST FACING PITCHES 12-14

arête joins talus
20 minutes of
3rd to summit

70' **15**

14 120'

5.6 cracks and corners
in center of arête

exposed
4th traverse

5.7
on south
side notch

13 100'

rappel 15'
or downclimb

12

escape gully

13 and 14 link with 60m rope

Ibrium Tower

15

14

13

12

11

incredible
splitter!

5.9
var.

white
quartz
veins

9

5.8

10

8

NORTHWEST FACING PITCHES 6-8

block with
slings

escape to the south
UP gully on four pitches
of 3rd and 4th class

8 100'

5.8

First Tower

Pitches 3-6 are
mostly 4th class with
occasional 5th class
moves. For best rock
and climbing, stay on
true arête. There
are many belay
options.

7 70'

6 100'

arête flattens

steep
loose
5.7
chim

escape to the south
on rappels down gully

First Tower

4th class
on arête

6 100'

downclimb
to notch

wild
5.7
exposed
traverse

5.6

notch

big
ledge

7 70'

5

gully

merging
arête

5 160'

4 160'

3 160'

broad
arête

gully
(don't climb
here)

NORTHWEST FACING PITCHES 10-12

Ibrium Tower

11 and 12 link
w/ 60m rope

40' **12**

big
block

steep and
sunstained
5.7

11 140'

5.6 in 20'
wide gully

edge
of
arête

don't go too high!
many off-route slings

80' **9**

descend 20'

3rd

150' **10**

Venusian
Blind

130' **2**

3rd

160' **1**

confident climbers
solo or simul-climb
Pitches 1-5

3rd

4th

steep
wall

traverse 200 feet
left on 3rd

200' drop
to talus

4th
chim

5.6
move

optional chimney start:
less snow than standard
start, but you may still
need crampons

snow

standard start
on snow—probably
need crampons

SP Parker and Bud Roper climbing the Sun Ribbon Arête. (Greg Epperson)

Sun Ribbon Arête

5.10a★★★★★

Time to climb route:	**8-10 hours**
Approach time:	**4 hours**
Descent time:	**5 hours**
Sun exposure:	**morning to afternoon**
Height of route:	**1500'**

This is one of the longest and most classic High Sierra arêtes. The route ascends a striking arête for 18 pitches and involves mostly 3rd and 4th class climbing with a number of short harder sections in the 5.6-5.10a range. This climb is long and even fast climbers require a full day. The Tyrolean Traverse, although not mandatory, is the logical way to pass a large gap in the arête and is the highlight of the route.

FA: Don Jensen, W. Miller, R. Schwartz, John Fischer, 1969.

History

By the late 1960s, Don Jensen was widely regarded around the Sierra as "The Man," the leading modern climber in the range. The 1969 season was to become his most famous one, mostly due to the "discovery" of a peak he and every other Palisade climber had hiked right past: Temple Crag. The winter of 1969 had been one of the heaviest of the century, and when the Mountaineering Guide Service guides went to arrange their usual basecamp below Mt. Gayley, the site was deep in snow. So they set up at Third Lake instead, a place where they would spend a lot of time looking up at Temple Crag. Up to this time, this peak was regarded as an impressive castle of unreliable rock, a consolation peak with loose gully routes, a mass that didn't measure up to the higher Palisades.

One morning early in that '69 season, young guide John Fischer gazed at Temple Crag as the sun skipped across its flying buttresses. He pointed out to Jensen that on those arêtes, in places at least, there were some pretty solid-looking facets with clean-looking cracks. Fischer was one of a few new Sierrans who had learned to climb not only on Sierra Club trips, but also in the new arena of smooth crack climbing, Yosemite Valley. Jensen immediately agreed there was some potential on Temple Crag, and soon afterward he took clients onto the biggest and most impressive of them.

There is some uncertainty about precisely when Jensen first started up the Sun Ribbon. Perhaps the first foray was when he went up with a fresh high-school graduate named Michael Graber, a teenager who had no idea he was going up on new ground, and who would launch from this start into a long and grand mountaineering career. Probably Jensen made a more complete ascent of the "lower Sun Ribbon" on July 29 with two other clients, W. Miller and R. Schwartz. In any case, Jensen marveled at how the route went so well, how great the rock was, and how the adjoining arêtes looked like good possibilities too. In both trips, when he came to a 30-foot-deep notch he arranged a rappel, but as he climbed up the opposite side he saw that it might be possible to lasso a horn and rig a Tyrolean Traverse across the gap. A few pitches later the climbing got hard again, and the conservative Jensen escaped on a ledge system into the chute to the left, and on to the top that way. He was ebullient though, for he knew he had found a whole new world on the northeast side of Temple Crag, and he would come to call the Sun Ribbon "perhaps the loveliest climb in the Palisades." With this introduction, Jensen would make it a weekly event during that August to take clients up onto one of Temple Crag's soaring fins.

Sun Ribbon Arête	Pitch	1	2	3	4	5	6	7	8	9	10	11	12	13	14	15	16	17	18
Free difficulty	≥5.10									●									
	5.9																		
	5.8															●			
	5.7	●		●	●	●	●												
	5.6								●										
	≤5.5		●					●	●			●	●	●	●	●		●	●

SUPERTOPO™

HIGH SIERRA CLIMBING: SUPERTOPOS

On September 2, he and Fischer teamed up to climb the Sun Ribbon in its entirety, at the same time as their fellow guides Carl Dreisbach and Pat Armstrong were making the first complete ascent of the adjacent Moon Goddess Arête. When Jensen and Fischer got to the 30-foot notch, they tossed a loop of rope across to a horn, pulled it tight, and then slid to the other side, yipping like crazed coyotes to the sky and to their compatriots. Jensen climbed well in his French LePhoque full-shank mountaineering boots, but when they reached the gendarme that had turned him away before, Fischer went for it with a new weapon on his feet: EBs. These snug and smooth *kletterschue* were essential to the Yosemite freeclimber, and this was probably their first use on a major new Sierra route. After that pitch, which they rated 5.8, they continued on the arête, still shouting for joy back and forth to Dreisbach and Armstrong, and reuniting with them on top with daylight to spare.

A few years later, a younger Bay Area climber, Brock Wagstaff, had a goal to do the Sun Ribbon in winter. He was thwarted in January 1978, but in February 1982 he came back with North America's premier alpinist, George Lowe. They arrived at Glacier Lodge during a cold snap, when the temperature was -10°F, but recalling Lowe's experience pioneering winter climbs in the Tetons they pressed on. Leading in plastic boots and with full packs, "bundled in all the clothes we had," they made it from the trailhead to the Tyrolean gap at dusk. They lassoed the horn and got across in time to huddle for the night under their tent on a tiny perch. The next day, in a biting wind, they resumed with "short bursts of climbing activity, followed by finger-warming sessions," and made the top with 15 minutes of daylight left. Into the night they kept going down, completing overnight from the car one of the Sierra's most brilliant winter ascents ever. When Wagstaff pried off his boots, he found that he had some serious frostbite, but luckily he would keep his toes.

– Andy Selters

Strategy

Get a dawn start. If climbing the route car-to-car in a day, get a predawn start. This route is rarely crowded.

Sun Ribbon Arête is accessed via the gully that divides it from Moon Goddess Arête. In early season, climb steep snow farther than you think into the gully where a large ledge system (impossible to see until you're there) leads to the first 5.7 pitch of the route. Bring an ice axe and crampons for this section. Later season or in low snow years it is usually possible to climb the moat between the snow and the rock up to the first pitch, avoiding snow altogether. This negates the need for ice axe/crampons. In certain light it is possible to see the first pitch from afar; look to the right of the approach gully for an area of light-colored rock that has darker, orange-ish rock to its right. All this is several hundred feet up and left of the toe of the Sun Ribbon Arête. The first pitch climbs strenuous 5.7 cracks where the orange rock and the lighter rock meet in a huge 30-foot left-facing corner.

Find your way to the first 5.7 pitch. (There have been several direct starts done in the 5.10 range). This leads to several hundred feet of 3rd class and the start of the first arête. The first five or six pitches are straightforward with many belay options and minor routefinding decisions. Eventually you'll find yourself at the top of the first arête, looking at the Tyrolean Traverse.

While this can be avoided, why would you do that? How often do you get to do a Tyrolean Traverse in real life? Plan this through the night before: a Tyrolean Traverse is a horizontal rappel. The first challenge is getting a loop of rope over the block on the other side of the span. Forget the lasso technique. The best method is to find one end of the rope, anchor it, and feed about 30 feet from this end into a pile by your right foot. Skip 5 to 6 feet and make a new pile of 30 or so feet on your left foot. Anchor this end near this point, too, just so loose rope doesn't go snaking off when you attempt a throw. Make sure both piles are feeding from their tops. Hold the rope so the loop of 5 to 6 feet between the piles droops down and almost touches your toes, each 30-foot pile is coiled loosely in a hand. Gauge wind direction and throw each loop of rope at the same time, one from each hand. You can probably do it in less than three tries.

Now you need to set up your horizontal rappel. Unanchor the rope, pass it through the fixed rap anchor and tie it off in such a way that a continuous loop is formed— tension it as best you can. I prefer to take the end of the rope, tie a bight, clip a 'biner, pass the other side of the rope through this, make a munter, tension, then tie it off with a mule knot. There are other systems that will also work.

Cross the span. A friction knot might be helpful getting up the other side if you weren't able to make your ropes tight. Once across you can make a real anchor or just leave what you have. Whatever you do you'll want to see if you can circulate the rope in the system and get the knot side back across. Otherwise your partner should undo it and then re-rig on your side of the span.

Several ways meet about 100 feet above the notch at the start of the pitch. The first heads left from the belay to a 5.10a handcrack with an off-route bolt. After the rattly crack climbing leads to the belay stance straight up. Or head out right from the belay past two fixed pins. A 5.10a face move gets you into a nice 5.9 hand crack. Loose 5.8 cracks and blocks lead to a good stance (same stance as other way). The belay at the end of this pitch is straight above the belay at the start of the pitch. If you go to the right, you can pull your rope up, drop it, haul packs, drop it, and safely belay the second. This doesn't work as well the left way.

Four more pitches of straightforward climbing lead to a rappel. From the rap, six or eight pitches with some 5.8 lead to the summit plateau.

Retreat

It is possible to retreat using one 50m or 60m rope. Retreat from the first part of the route by rappelling left into the gully. From the end of this horizontal section below the crux Pitch 11, it is easy to do a diagonal rappel left into the gully. Forty-five minutes of 4th class lead to the summit plateau.

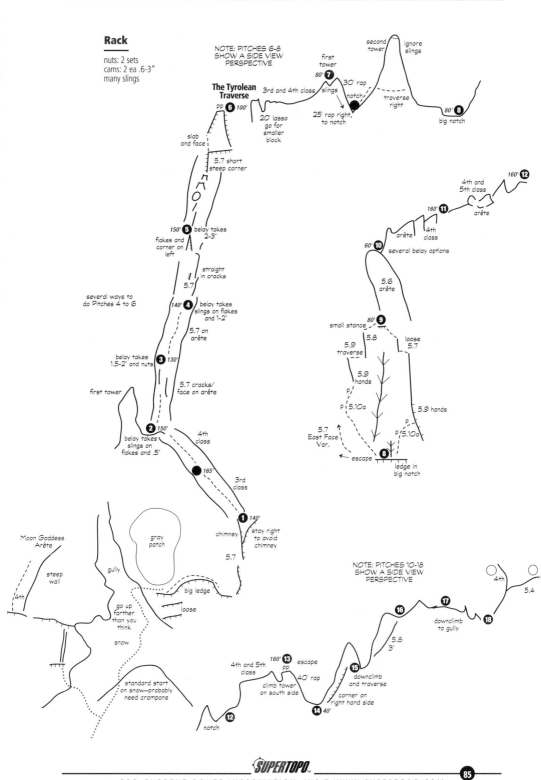

Rack

nuts: 2 sets
cams: 2 ea .6-3"
many slings

NOTE: PITCHES 6-8
SHOW A SIDE VIEW
PERSPECTIVE

second tower

ignore slings

first tower

80' ⑦

30' rap notch

25' rap right, to notch

traverse right

80' ⑧

big notch

The Tyrolean Traverse

3rd and 4th class

slings

PP ⑥ 100'

20' lasso go for smaller block

slab and face

5.7 short steep corner

160' ⑫

4th and 5th class

arête

160' ⑪

150' ⑤ belay takes 2-3"

flakes and corner on left

straight in cracks

5.7

arête

4th class

60' ⑩

several belay options

several ways to do Pitches 4 to 6

140' ④ belay takes slings on flakes and 1-2"

5.7 on arête

5.6 arête

belay takes 1.5-2" and nuts

③ 130'

5.7 cracks/ face on arête

small stance 80' ⑨

5.9 traverse

5.8

loose 5.7

first tower

② 150'

belay takes slings on flakes and .5"

4th class

5.9 hands

P

P 5.10a

5.9 hands

165'

3rd class

5.7 East Face Var.

P

P 5.10a

① 140'

chimney

stay right to avoid chimney

escape

⑧

ledge in big notch

5.7

Moon Goddess Arête

gray patch

steep wall

gully

4th

go up farther than you think

big ledge

loose

NOTE: PITCHES 10-18
SHOW A SIDE VIEW
PERSPECTIVE

4th

5.4

snow

⑯

⑰

downclimb to gully

⑱

standard start on snow—probably need crampons

4th and 5th class

160' ⑬ PP

escape

40' rap

climb tower on south side

5.8 3'

⑮ downclimb and traverse

corner on right hand side

⑭ 40'

⑫

notch

Mt. Goode

As you hike along Long Lake toward Bishop Pass, Mt. Goode (13,085') is hard to ignore and its striking north buttress begs to be climbed. It is the typical Sierra peak with a mixture of great and loose rock, but has atypical steepness and exposure. Because the North Buttress is often shaded and rises from a small glacier, it has a dark and ominous feel that makes climbing it a great alpine adventure.

Chris McNamara

Approach

Take Highway 168 out of Bishop until you reach a sign that directs you to South Lake. Take this left-hand turn and continue all the way to the South Lake parking lot.

The approach is about 5 miles (3.5 miles on trail and 1.5 miles cross-country), takes 3-4 hours, and gains about 2,200 feet in elevation. Relative to other Sierra approaches, the hike to Mt. Goode is straightforward. Note: You do not descend to the base of the route, so only carry what you will need on the climb.

Follow the Bishop Pass Trail about 3 miles to the far (south) end of Long Lake. Mt. Goode becomes visible once you reach Long Lake. (If you reach Spearhead Lake, you've gone too far.) Leave the trail at the south end of Long Lake and hike on mellow cross-country toward Mt. Goode for about 0.5 mile to Margaret Lake. Walk to the west end of Margaret Lake (last water). Another mile of rough cross-country leads you to the base of the climb. Hike to the slabby buttress on the right side of a huge, steep moraine. From the base, follow its left edge on fairly solid sand and talus. Once on the top of this moraine you will

be faced with the routefinding crux of the approach. Instead of heading directly toward Mt. Goode, head southwest and stay in the gully on boulders until you are pretty much parallel with the route. At this point, head south over the last steep section of the moraine to the snow field at the base of the peak. Stay left up talus as far as you can go as the snow/ice can be bulletproof—especially in late season. Find divets and rocks frozen into the snow to ease the walk to the base of the route. Trekking poles will help, but an ice axe may be necessary. There are a few direct starts in between the huge arêtes, but we recommend starting on the right side of these arêtes on the slab—mainly because you then don't have to belay on the snow!

Descent

This descent is about as dreamy as they come with sand for the first 1.5 miles and great trail for the last 4 miles. It takes about 2-3 hours and is way more mellow than the approach.

From the summit, drop down southeast (toward Mt. Agassiz) on talus that quickly turns to fun, sandy trail. When the sand starts to flatten out, contour around left aiming for the land bridge between Saddlerock and Bishop Lakes. Eventually the flat sand ends at a long, steep sand and brush slope. Look for trails and aim for the south shore of Saddlerock Lake. Take a nice swim if you desire, then follow the trail on the south then east shore and merge with the Bishop Pass Trail. Follow the trail back to the car.

The approach as seen from 5 minutes before Margaret Lake.

Backcountry Camping

Many climbers camp at Long Lake the night before the climb. Long Lake is about 1 hour from the trailhead, about 1.5 hours from the start of the climb, and offers incredible views of Mt. Goode. You will need an overnight permit (see "Backcountry Camping Permits" in Introduction, page 24). Due to high demand, you may need to reserve yours at least a month in advance.

The descent as seen from the summit.

North Buttress 5.9★★★

Time to climb route: **6-8 hours**

Approach time: **3-4 hours**

Descent time: **2-3 hours**

Sun exposure: **partial sun**

Height of route: **800'**

The relatively straightforward approach, beautiful setting and steep, dramatic buttress add to the appeal of this route. The North Buttress is the classic High Sierra route—loose and exposed in places. There are some great pitches, but also some loose rock. This is a good route to do after you have climbed some of the more classic 5.9s such as Fishhook Arête on Mt. Russell. You should be a solid 5.9 leader as the crux pitch, although well-protected, is stout. Because there is a runout 5.9 face traverse, the follower as well as the leader should be aware of the potential for a nasty pendulum fall.

FA: John Fischer, Dennis Hennek, Jay Jensen, TM Herbert, 9/74.

Strategy

Most people do this route car-to-car in a big day. You can also hike up to Long or Margaret Lake, camp, and do the climb and hike out the next day. Because the route is north-facing it can be cold in late-season and the snow at the base may be treacherous. Bring warm layers and a hat. It is doubtful that you will see crowds on this route. But if you do, with all the loose rock on the route it may be dangerous with other climbers above you. A 50m rope is sufficient for this climb.

Pitch 3 is the first crux and is serious for both the follower and the leader. From the second belay, downclimb 15 feet and step on a large block with loose flakes above it. Climb left on runout 5.8 face to a piton and then step down around the arête (5.9). Downclimb on small edges to a ledge inside a chimney. From here, you can either climb the 5.8 chimney halfway and then move left onto the face or step around left onto the 5.9 face right away from the ledge—both options are runout.

The next crux, Pitch 5, is well-protected, but a bit insecure and stout. From the notch, climb into double cracks and use finger jams and stemming.

Retreat

Once you are done with the first pitch, you will have to rappel straight down and find your own anchors and leave gear.

North Buttress	Pitch	1	2	3	4	5	6	7	8	9
Free difficulty	≥5.10									
	5.9			●		●				●
	5.8	●	●				●			
	5.7								●	
	5.6							●		
	≤5.5				●					

Rack

nuts: 1 set
cams: 1-2 ea .6-3.5"

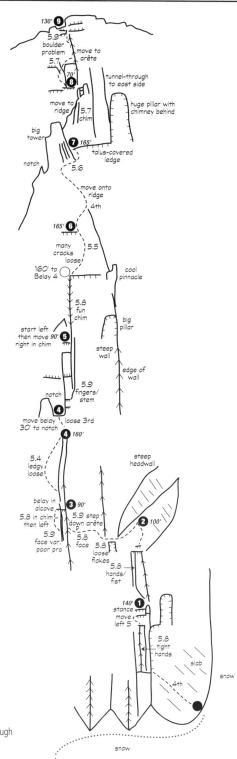

130' **9**

5.9
boulder
problem   move to
arête
5.7

tunnel-through
to east side

70' **8**

move to   huge pillar with
ridge   5.7   chimney behind
chim

big
tower   **7** 165'

notch   talus-covered
ledge

5.6

move onto
ridge
4th

165' **6**

many
cracks
loose   5.5

160' to   ◯   cool
Belay 4   pinnacle

5.8
fun   big
chim   pillar

start left
then move 90' **5**
right in chim   steep
wall
edge of
wall
5.9
notch   fingers/
stem

4

move belay   loose 3rd
30' to notch

4 160'
steep
headwall
5.4
ledgy
loose

belay in   **2** 100'
alcove   **3** 90'
5.8 in chim   5.9 step
then left   down arête

5.9   5.8   5.8
face var.   face   loose
poor pro   flakes

5.8
hands/
fist

140' **1**
stance
move
left 5'

5.8
tight
hands

slab   snow

4th

snow

Sarah Felchlin approaches the tunnel-through
on Pitch 8. (Chris McNamara)

Bear Creek Spire

Flanked in all directions with steep faces and good rock, Bear Creek Spire (13,720') is the most classic climbing peak in the Rock Creek area. Nearly every face requires some 5th class climbing and the true summit itself requires a 5.6 R mantel.

One of the main attractions is the ease of access to the peak and a moderate and beautiful approach hike through Little Lakes Valley. The parking lot is at 10,260 feet giving you a head start to your climb and putting you instantly in a beautiful alpine environment.

Approach

From U.S. 395, take the Tom's Place Exit. Tom's Place has a restaurant, bar, lodging, and some groceries, but no gas. Drive up the Rock Creek Road and park at Mosquito Flat (and yes, as the name implies, the mosquitoes are terrible in early summer). Note that the road is closed 6 miles before Mosquito Flat from as early as November to as late as June (depending on the snow year). Check the SuperTopo web site for road conditions.

The approach takes most climbers 3 to 4 hours (double times with heavy pack) from Mosquito Flat to the base of the climb and involves 3.5 miles on the main trail, 2.5 miles on climbers' trails and cross-country travel, and gains about 2,500 feet in elevation. The trailhead is located at 10,260 feet making it the highest access point in the Sierra Nevada and one of the highest public access roads in the United States.

From Mosquito Flat, hike the Little Lakes Valley Trail for about 3.5 miles and 1 hour to just before Morgan Pass. This popular trail is the remnants of an old mining road that once ran from Tom's Place to Rovana. Turn off the main trail after a wooden footbridge that crosses a creek and follow a well-worn climbers' trail for 5 minutes to Gem Lakes. From here, the climbers' trail only appears intermittently. Hike up left (southeast) a steep talus drainage to an unnamed lake and continue southwest to Dade Lake (last water) and then walk directly toward Bear Creek Spire.

For the North Arête route, walk directly toward the striking arête/buttress. The last hundred feet leading to the base of the climb involve climbing relatively steep snow. This snow, because it receives first

North Arête

Northeast Ridge

Chris McNamara

light, is usually soft enough
to kick steps in with regular
hiking shoes. However, in
cold conditions in the late
fall, crampons and an ice axe
may be necessary.

For the Northeast Ridge
route, walk to the saddle at
the base of the Northeast
Ridge.

Spring Approach Conditions

It is not uncommon for snow
to cover the approach from
Gem Lakes to the base of the
climb until early July. Make
sure the snow is freezing at
night and start hiking early.
If the snow does not freeze
at night and/or you hike
in the afternoon once the
snow heats up, the approach
will be a slushy post-holing
nightmare. Bring snowshoes
or skis if approaching on
snow in the afternoon.
Snowshoes are also helpful
for the descent.

The Bear Creek Spire approach from the summit ridge. This photo shows early
summer approach conditions and the frozen Dade Lake is hard to see.

Treasure Lakes Alternate Approach

An alternate approach leaves the main trail
at the south end of Long Lake and follows a
climbers'/fishermen's trail to Treasure Lakes
and eventually joins the approach described
above at Dade Lake. This alternate approach
is not recommended because it requires
trickier routefinding, is slower, and involves
more talus travel.

Descent

It takes 3-5 hours to get from the summit back to Mosquito Flat. From the summit, make a 50-foot rappel from slings or downclimb the way you came up. Hike to the northwest, first downclimbing 3rd class, then walking on talus and a sandy trail, and finally walking on sand to a low-point in the northwest ridge. From here walk through a notch then downclimb 3rd and 4th class or rappel down to the snow. The snow is steep, but usually soft in the afternoon and perfect for glissading. Head toward Dade Lake and reverse the approach.

Backcountry Camping

Many climbers camp at Dade Lake the night before the climb. Dade Lake is just 45 minutes from the base of Bear Creek Spire and offers incredible views of the North Arête and Northeast Ridge. Another option is to camp at Gem Lakes. You will need an overnight permit. See "Backcountry Camping Permits" in Introduction, page 24.

If you need to camp near the trailhead before the climb, stay at Mosquito Flat Trailhead Campground. This free walk-in campground is only for persons with an overnight backcountry permit, and the stay limit is one night.

GPS Coordinates

Mosquito Flat:
  37° 26' 100", 118° 44' 813"
Gem Lakes turnoff:
  37° 23' 560", 118° 45' 289"
After steep talus above Gem Lakes:
  37° 23' 192", 118° 45' 330"
Approaching Dade Lake:
  37° 22' 965", 118° 45' 569"
Southwest end of Dade Lake:
  37° 22' 730", 118° 45' 870"
Between Dade Lake and routes:
  37° 22' 360", 118° 45' 933"
Steep snow at North Arête start:
  37° 22' 284", 118° 46' 010"
Second belay on North Arête:
  37° 22' 167", 118° 46' 025"
Start of Northeast Ridge Route:
  37° 22' 263", 118° 45' 788"
Summit of Bear Creek Spire:
  37° 22' 066", 118° 46' 056"

Descent
Between summit and notch:
  37° 22' 156", 118° 46' 146"
Notch in Northwest Ridge:
  37° 22' 224", 118° 46' 191"

The start of the descent as seen from 200 feet below the summit.

Chris McNamara

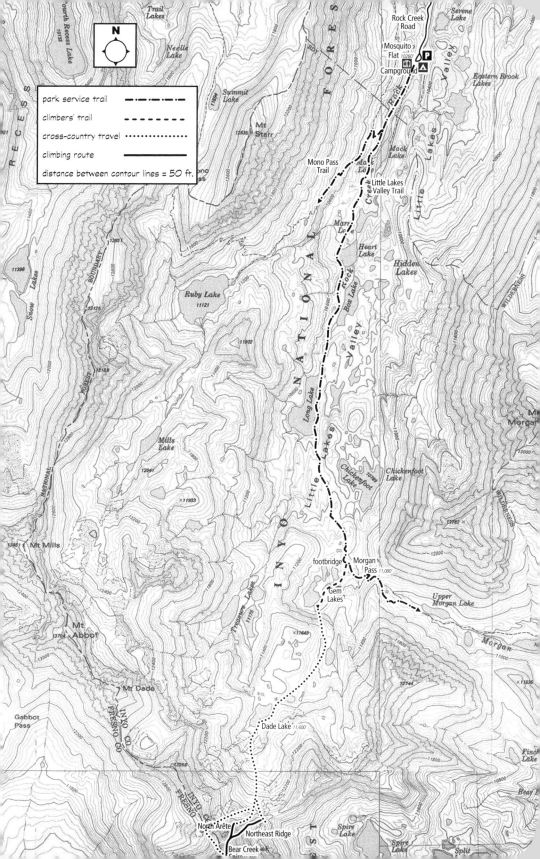

Map Legend

park service trail	—·—·—·—
climbers' trail	– – – – –
cross-country travel	··········
climbing route	———————

distance between contour lines = 50 ft.

N

Labels on map:

Rock Creek Road
Serene Lake
Mosquito Flat 10260
Campground
Eastern Brook Lakes
Rock Creek Road
Trail Lakes
Fourth Recess Lake 10732
Needle Lake
Summit Lake
Mt Starr 12835
Mack Lake
Mono Pass Trail
Little Lakes Valley Trail
Little Lakes
Marsh Lake
Heart Lake
Hidden Lakes
Ruby Lake 11121
Box Lake
Rock Creek
Little Lakes Valley
Long Lake
Mills Lake 12041
Mt Morgan 13000
×11933
Chickenfoot Lake 10789
Chickenfoot Lake
12782×
Mt Mills 13451
BOUNDARY 13125
13148
Treasure Lakes 11776
footbridge
Morgan Pass 11080
Mt Abbot 13704
Gem Lakes
Upper Morgan Lake
Morgan Creek
12744
×13535
×11645
Mt Dade
Gabbot Pass
Dade Lake 11600
INYO NATIONAL FOREST
INYO CO FRESNO CO
Finger Lake
13768
Spire Lake
North Arête
Northeast Ridge
Bear Creek Spire
Spire Lake
Split
Bear Lake
RECESS
WILDERNESS

North Arête 5.8★★★★

Time to climb route: **5-8 hours**

Approach time: **3-4 hours**

Descent time: **3-5 hours**

Sun exposure: **partial, all day or none**

Height of route: **800'**

The North Arête takes the most compelling line on Bear Creek Spire. The climb is typical for a Sierra route: lots of cracks, broken rock, and mostly face climbing and stemming with a few mandatory hand jams. Both cruxes involve steep stemming on awkward large flakes. The climb is easily divided in two halves. The first half climbs a striking arête/pillar with steep 5.7 and 5.8 sections separated by 4th class. The second half ascends an exposed 4th class ridge. Because only the first half is visible from the base, many climbers underestimate the length of the climb.

FA: Galen Rowell, Jeanne Neale, 8/71.

History

For Galen Rowell, the summer of 1971 seems like the year his frenetic drive found its stride on mountain granite. He had been climbing in Yosemite for a few seasons, and he started on a campaign to apply advanced Yosemite techniques to walls in wilderness settings and on high peaks. In the spring, he climbed new routes on the Fuller Buttes, and he teamed with Doug Robinson to finish the first ascent of the Smokestack on Wheeler Crest. In June, he and Chris Jones put up spectacular routes on both Angel Wings and Mt. Russell. In July, he, Jones, and Tony Qamar went to the Bugaboos and climbed the huge west face of the North Howser Tower. In August, he was back in Yosemite, and there "a big red flag went up when I saw climbers far more talented than myself unwilling to test in the nearby wilderness those skills acquired in this fair-weather womb... I decided to go to Bear Creek Spire, alone."

He arranged to traverse the peak by caching a bicycle at the Mosquito Flat trailhead for his return, and then hiking in from Pine Creek. He belayed himself up the first ascent of the peak's south face, and in waning light he made his way down the original route to a bivouac below Bear Creek Spire's north aspect. In the morning he saw in profile a moderate-looking spine of solid, clean rock—the north arête—and he decided to come back for it.

The following June, Rowell found a date for the route, Berkeley neighbor Jeanne Neale. They hiked in to a camp at Dade Lake, and in the morning they packed a hefty range of pitons, one rope, and their rock shoes. The granite proved to be as solid as it looked, and with Rowell leading all the pitches they worked up the slabs, corners, and cracks. By 11 a.m. they were laughing on the summit.

– Andy Selters

Strategy

In June, the route receives sun all day. In later months, the route is often shaded all day. The route can be freezing in September and October (bring warm clothes). If climbing the route car-to-car, get a predawn start. The route is popular so expect some waiting behind slower parties. It is possible to pass slower parties on most pitches by wandering to either side of the standard route. A 60m rope is not mandatory but will let you do the upper half of the route in one less pitch if you stretch every pitch out.

North Arête	Pitch	1	2	3	4	5	6	7	8	9	10
Free difficulty	≥5.10										
	5.9										
	5.8					●					
	5.7	●	●								
	5.6										
	≤5.5			●	●		●	●	●	●	●

The crux Pitch 5 involves steep and awkward 5.8 flakes. Some climbers chimney between flakes, some use offwidth technique, and some stem. This section is particularly hard with a backpack. Above the 5.8, be careful of knocking rocks down the loose 5.6 gully/chimney, especially if there are climbers below.

The second half of the climb involves mostly 4th class on the exposed arête/ridge. Stay on the arête/ridge when possible because not only is the climbing better, but it is often easier than climbing the northeast face down and left.

It is possible to follow the true ridge all the way to the summit but the last section is 5.9 and most climbers traverse onto the west face for an easy scramble to the top. The final move onto the summit block is unprotectable 5.6. Using a rope for this section won't keep you from injury but may offer some "psychological protection."

Retreat

To retreat from the first pitch, walk left (east) to the gully, or rappel. To retreat from Pitches 2-5, rappel to the right (west) into the snow gully. There may be some fixed slings to rappel from, however, be prepared to leave your own gear. If retreating from above Pitch 5, consider rappelling and scrambling down the Northeast Ridge route to the left (east). An extra rope for retreat is not necessary because rappelling longer than half a rope length is likely to result in stuck ropes.

Chris McNamara

Rack

nuts: 1-2 sets
cams: 1 ea .5-3"
many slings

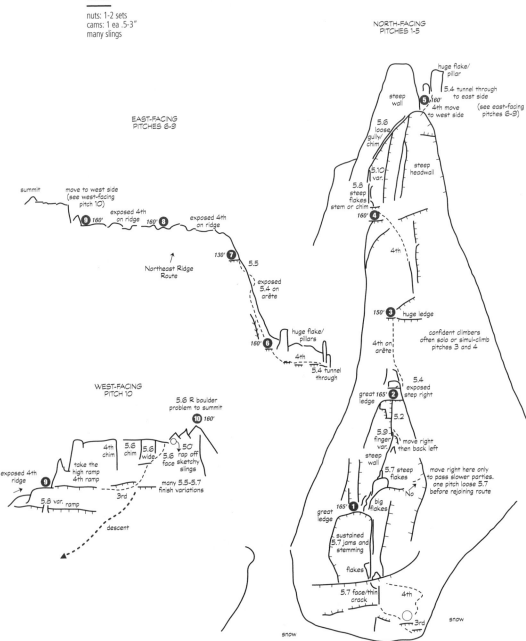

NORTH-FACING
PITCHES 1-5

huge flake/
pillar

steep
wall

5.4 tunnel through
to east side

5 160'

4th move
to west side

(see east-facing
pitches 6-9)

5.6
loose
gully/
chim

steep
headwall

5.10
var.

5.8
steep
flakes
stem or chim

160' 4

4th

150' 3   huge ledge

confident climbers
often solo or simul-climb
pitches 3 and 4

4th on
arête

5.4
exposed
step right

great 165' 2
ledge

5.2

5.9
finger
var.

move right
then back left

steep
wall

5.7 steep
flakes

move right here only
to pass slower parties.
one pitch loose 5.7
before rejoining route

No

great 165' 1
ledge

big
flakes

sustained
5.7 jams and
stemming

flakes

5.7 face/thin
crack

4th

3rd

snow

snow

EAST-FACING
PITCHES 6-9

summit

move to west side
(see west-facing
pitch 10)

9 160'   160' 8

exposed 4th
on ridge

exposed 4th
on ridge

130' 7   5.5

Northeast Ridge
Route

exposed
5.4 on
arête

160' 6

huge flake/
pillars

4th

5.4 tunnel
through

WEST-FACING
PITCH 10

5.6 R boulder
problem to summit

10 160'

4th
chim

5.6
chim

5.6
wide

5.6
face

50'
rap off
sketchy
slings

take the
high ramp
4th ramp

many 5.5-5.7
finish variations

exposed 4th
ridge

9

3rd

5.8 var. ramp

descent

Northeast Ridge 5.5★★★★

Time to climb route:	**3-6 hours**
Approach time:	**3-4 hours**
Descent time:	**3-5 hours**
Sun exposure:	**partial, all day or none**
Height of route:	**1,200′**

Many people debate which Bear Creek Spire route is more classic: the Northeast Ridge or North Arête? The Northeast Ridge follows a striking ridgeline while the North Arête ascends the most dramatic arête on the face. Both routes are awesome and your choice of which route to climb will be more about whether you want sustained technical climbing (North Arête) or mostly 4th class terrain (Northeast Ridge). While in the past this route has been rated 4th class, we call it 5.5 because we do not know anyone who has done the route and not encountered more than a few 5th class sections.

FA: Norman Clyde, 5/32.

History

Not until 1931 did Norman Clyde visit Bear Creek Spire, the peak he called "perhaps the least known of the finer peaks of the southern Sierra Nevada." This was four years after he'd been removed from his teaching career and the fifth year he'd been able to extend his climbing season into the fall. Despite September storms that had left a blanket of new snow on high peaks, in early October Clyde headed up Pine Creek to camp, probably at Bear Lake. Since 1916 a few miners had poked around here, but now, during The Depression, few visited this area. The Spire's first ascent had come in 1923, when a youthful Hermann Ulrichs had deviated from a scout troop outing and climbed it from the west. Since then Clyde figured there had been five other ascents by that route.

Clyde figured to hike counter-clockwise around the north side of the peak, and climb it by the original route too. However, when he got under the peak's northeast face, he pulled out his binoculars and decided on the spot that he saw terrain for a new and expedient route. He charted a course angling up and right toward the summit. Employing some classic mixed climbing, chopping steps up icy chutes and brushing snow off of granite ribs, he reached the top with just enough daylight to descend by the original route.

Over the winter he decided that the peak was worthy enough to go back in the spring and repeat his new route. In May, he hiked in even though an unusually heavy snowpack was not even half melted. Approaching again from Morgan Creek, he found his objective thoroughly white, and he decided that his route was too avalanche-prone. He wisely looked for and found a rocky arête, though, to the right. A steep cliff at the bottom looked to be the only serious obstacle, but he quickly worked a way through this by scrambling up a chimney and cutting back left onto the arête. He climbed along the crest of the broken spine for a distance, then steep blocks turned him onto its left flank where he could connect high ledges. Near the summit he returned to the arête's crest, but a typical spring gale forced him to keep to a more sheltered finish on its east flank.

On this final traverse he came to a ledge that dead-ended at a narrow chimney, and the impasse bid him to shed his pack and set it up for hauling. But as he uncoiled his line, he heard a noise and turned to see his whole kit sliding away. It tumbled off and skidded down snowslopes, and then launched over cliffs and disappeared. He kept watching for it, and, "far below it reappeared, bounding down over another snow slope some 500 feet in width, and finally coming to rest at the edge of a cliff. 'That's the end of camera, binoculars, etc.,' I thought." After tagging the top in the driving wind, Clyde descended the same northeast arête, hoping to collect the remains of his gear. However, he couldn't find a reasonable way to its perch, and he returned to camp.

The following day he climbed back up the cliff at the start of the northeast arête, to where he could traverse over to his pack. What had looked like scattered rocks he found to be "various items of my equipment, most of them in a more or less damaged condition…One lens was missing from the binoculars…[but camera] lenses and shutter speed seemed intact, and an automatic pistol, carried for collecting purposes, was apparently none the worse for the thousand-foot combination of drops and glissades…

"Being only about a thousand feet below the summit…I climbed [Bear Creek Spire] for the third time, finding the day much more pleasant than the preceding." Clyde noticed that the headwall to the east of the northeast arête was also climbable, and he figured that if snow conditions had been safe he would have completed a third new route.

– *Andy Selters*

Strategy

The best time to climb the route is July through October. In late May and June snow covers the upper route forcing you to climb the true ridge.

Either start at the true saddle at the bottom of the ridge or traverse a few hundred feet up. The first few hundred yards ascend 3rd class to the first tower where the difficulties begin and remain sustained to the summit. In general, the true ridge has better and more sustained climbing. If you stay left of the ridge, prepare to wander.

Once you reach the summit ridge and merge with the North Arête route, stay on the true ridge when possible because not only is the climbing better, but it is often easier than climbing the northeast face down and left.

It is possible to follow the true ridge all the way to the summit, but the last section is 5.9 and most climbers traverse onto the west face for an easy scramble to the top. The final move onto the summit block is unprotectable 5.6. Using a rope for this section won't keep you from injury but may offer some "psychological protection."

Retreat

To retreat, rappel and downclimb the route. Once on the last few exposed ridge pitches, it is easier to finish the climb than rappel the route. An extra rope for retreat is not necessary because rappelling longer than 100 feet is likely to result in stuck ropes.

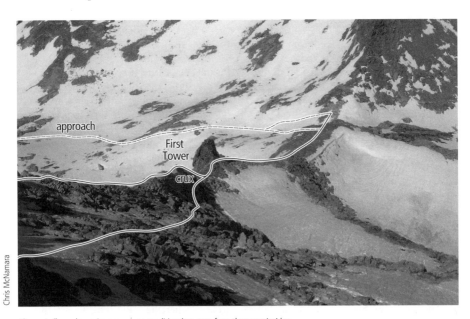

Chris McNamara

The route (here shown in snowy June conditions) as seen from the summit ridge.

Rack

nuts: 1-2 sets
cams: 1 ea .5-1" (optional)
many slings

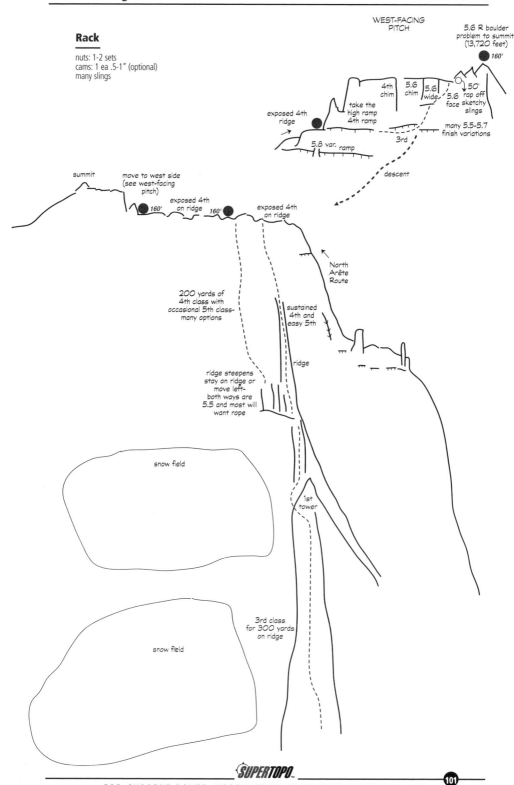

WEST-FACING PITCH

5.6 R boulder problem to summit (13,720 feet) 160'

4th chim

5.6 chim

5.6 wide

5.6 face

50' rap off sketchy slings

exposed 4th ridge

take the high ramp 4th ramp

many 5.5-5.7 finish variations

5.8 var. ramp

3rd

descent

summit

move to west side (see west-facing pitch)

exposed 4th on ridge 160'

160'

exposed 4th on ridge

North Arête Route

200 yards of 4th class with occasional 5th class- many options

sustained 4th and easy 5th

ridge

ridge steepens stay on ridge or move left- both ways are 5.5 and most will want rope

snow field

1st tower

3rd class for 300 yards on ridge

snow field

Laurel Mountain

From a distance, the Northeast Face of Laurel Mountain (11,812') looks like a massive, unappealing pile of choss. While that is mostly true, one gully snakes up surprisingly good rock. With only a 45-minute approach, this is one of the High Sierra's most easily accessed peaks.

Approach

From U.S. 395, take the Convict Lake Road located 10 miles north of Tom's Place and 4.4 miles south of Highway 203 (the turnoff for Mammoth Lakes). Drive 2 miles and park at Convict Lake.

The approach takes 45 minutes, is 1.5 miles long, and gains about 700 feet in elevation.

From the parking area, follow the Convict Canyon Trail along the north shore of Convict Lake and then up switchbacks for about 1.5 miles until you begin to cross light-colored talus/scree. Move up the talus to the obvious start of the gully.

Descent

There are three descent options: 1) the long, mellow way down the Laurel Creek Trail and Convict Canyon Trail back to Convict Lake; 2) the shortest, mellow way down the Laurel Creek Trail to the Sherwin Creek Road (best way); and 3) the short, grueling way down the North Ridge. All options are described below.

Laurel Creek Trail to Convict Canyon Trail

This is the longest descent option and may take as long as climbing the route. It is about 10 miles long and takes about 4 hours. From the summit, walk west and parallel to the North Ridge. Gradually contour west taking the path of least resistance and hook around west to the Laurel Lake Trail. Walk southeast for about 3 miles to Lake Dorothy at which point the trail becomes the Convict Canyon Trail. Continue another 7 miles to Convict Lake.

above: The numbers above correspond to the text in the Strategy section on page 107.
opposite: Brad Goya nears the shattered red rock mid-route. The first red vein and Convict Lake are visible below.
(Chris McNamara)

Laurel Creek Trail to Sherwin Creek Road

This descent is 5 miles long and takes about 2 hours. It is the most straightforward option but requires shuttling a car by driving U.S. 395 to Sherwin Creek Road. Drive 1.5 miles and pull off at the Laurel Lakes Turnoff. From here it is 4.5 miles to Laurel Lakes along a very rough, abandoned mining road. If you feel up for it and have 4WD, park at Laurel Lakes or at any pull-out 3-4 miles up the road. (When you emerge from the descent, you may have to hike up the road to your car.)

From the summit, walk west and parallel to the North Ridge. Gradually contour west taking the path of least resistance to the Laurel Creek Trail, which is an old mining/4WD road. It is about 1.5 miles from the summit to the 4WD road. If your car is parked at the Sherwin Creek Road, you will have 4 more miles to hike (unless a kind fisherman gives you a ride).

North Ridge

This descent is about 4 miles long and takes 2-3 hours. From the summit walk west and parallel to the north ridge for about a mile staying near the ridgeline. After about a mile, the ridge becomes more pronounced and a large cirque is visible to the north. (Don't go down the cirque or you will be bushwacking through very thick brush.) Move onto the ridgeline for a few hundred yards until you can drop down a scree and sand gully to the east. If you drop down a scary-looking gully, you probably dropped down too soon and should continue on the ridge. Once in the main gully steep scree turns into steep sand then some small shrubs. Intermittent trail leads all the way back to Convict Canyon Trail to within a hundred yards of the start of the climbing route.

GPS Coordinates

Parking area: 37° 35' 716", 118° 51' 103"
Leave Convict Canyon Trail:
  37° 35' 028", 118° 52' 331"
Start of route: 37° 35' 028", 118° 52' 520"
Summit: 37° 34' 822", 118° 53' 427"
Northeast Ridge Descent 1:
  37° 35' 277", 118° 53' 093"
Northeast Ridge Descent 2:
  37° 35' 300", 118° 52' 832"
Northeast Ridge Descent 3:
  37° 35' 177", 118° 52' 497"

A view of the climbing route from the approach trail. The summit and upper half of the route are not visible. (Numbers in the photo correspond to the text on page 107.)

Chris McNamara

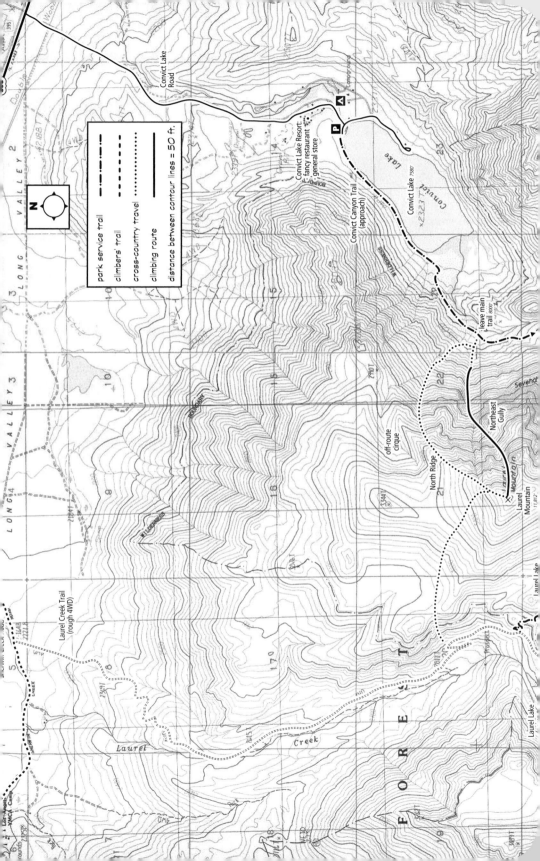

N

LONG VALLEY 2

LONG VALLEY 3

LONG VALLEY 3

Convict Lake Road

Convict Lake Resort:
fancy restaurant
general store

Convict Canyon Trail
(approach)

Convict Lake 7580'
×2323 Convict Lake

leave main
trail 8000'

off-route
cirque

North Ridge

Northeast
Gully

Laurel Mountain

Laurel Mountain
×11,812'

Sevehah

Laurel Creek Trail
(rough 4WD)

Laurel   Creek

FOREST

Laurel Lake

Laurel Lake

WILDERNESS
BOUNDARY

WILDERNESS

WILDERNESS
BOUNDARY

XMCA Camp

park service trail

climbers' trail

cross-country travel

climbing route

distance between contour lines = 50 ft.

Northeast Gully 5.2★★★

Time to climb route: **4-6 hours**

Approach time: **45 minutes**

Descent time: **2-4 hours**

Sun exposure: **sunrise to afternoon**

Height of route: **3,500'**

Ascending the wild gully that winds its way up Laurel Mountain is a test of endurance and routefinding skills. If you don't mind some bad rock, getting off route, and lots of hiking, then this climb/scramble is a true adventure. Atop the summit, you will be rewarded with an awesome view of Mono Lake to the north.

This route is huge and involves over a mile of 3rd and 4th class climbing. From a distance, the line is clear. Once on the climb, however, you enter a maze of gullies where it is easy to get lost. Think of this route as part Sierra scramble and part canyoneering expedition.

The rock in the main gully is mostly a pumice stone-like substrate that offers a clean and enjoyable passage through the surrounding sea of decaying loose choss. Along the way, various types of red, white, gray, and black rock enter the gully making this a geologist's dream climb.

FA: John Mendenhall, James Van Patten, 9/30.

History

Through the 1920s Sierra climbers knew little about rope techniques. It was the norm for Sierra Club tigers to work their way unroped up steep and seriously exposed terrain with no more security than careful bravado, an occasional shoulder stand, and perhaps a handline to aid a descent. Seeing an accident waiting to happen, some members began to talk about the need to learn and use the Alpine methods of rope safety. The first to put this attitude into practice was John Mendenhall, and the first Sierra climb he did this on was the northeast chute of Laurel Mountain.

He teamed up with fellow Angeleno James Van Patten on September 7, 1930. Mendenhall wrote that for the first thousand feet they "were roped, moved one at a time, and employed the belays…Fifty feet of rope between climbers is sufficient upon this climb."

Pitons had not yet come to California, so their belay methods were of the most traditional sort, with the belayer finding a position as firmly braced as possible, and running the rope probably over a shoulder. It was well-emphasized at this time that this method provides an adequate catch should the second slip, but a leader's fall would endanger the whole party, and thus, "the leader does not fall." After overcoming the route's steep ground, the pair continued to the top unroped. After enjoying the view they descended northward and then veered toward Convict Lake where "a broken-field run down these slopes [provided] a fitting end to a fine day."

During the heavy snow years of the early 1980s, extreme skier Walter Rosenthal made the first ski descent of this route. In 1996, Peter Croft revived interest in it when he got one of his irresistible urges to climb something and *now*—at about 4 p.m. He scanned maps, decided to try Laurel and drove to Convict Lake. Needing to hustle to beat nightfall, he reached the summit just an hour and 48 minutes after leaving his car. He came down smiling, calling it "one of the best routes in the Sierra."

– *Andy Selters*

Strategy

Start climbing early. Because the route is east-facing, it is often hot on a summer morning. There are few crowds.

Most climbers solo this route or bring a 100-foot rope for just a few short, steep sections. It is best to wear sticky rubber approach shoes, but if you don't have approach shoes, bring climbing shoes for a few short sections.

During the winter, this route fills with snow. When the snow melts in the summer, the route is covered in a layer of dirt. Wait until a few thunderstorms have washed the dirt off the rock—usually in July.

From a distance, the route is obvious: Start in the main gully and follow it as it bends left to a point 200 feet left of the summit of Laurel Mountain. Once you are on the route, however, you realize the topography is complex—it often feels like you are in a vertical maze. This quality adds to both the route's seriousness and adventure. Study the route carefully from the parking area and from the approach before you start climbing.

Finding the start is easy: Get in the big trough and go up. The first few hundred yards are some of the most demanding and involve short 5.2 bulges (some may want a belay).

Note: Numbers below refer to all photos.

A few hundred yards from the start, you will come to a **fork** (1). Stay right up red rock. However, from this point on, when in doubt, stay left.

After another few hundred feet, the trough opens up. Stay left as you cross an amazing 80-foot-wide, 2,000-plus-foot-long **vein of red rock** (2) that sweeps from one side of the gully all the way to the other side. A gray slab leads into a 300-foot-wide band of **broken red rock** (3), which forms again into a distinct gully.

ATTENTION: The instructions that follow are about as useful as a ouija board. It is nearly impossible to give an accurate description. Everyone does the upper route differently. In general, trend left and avoid crap rock when possible.

From the broken red rock, many people become disoriented and assume the route ascends the big, cool-looking gray slabs above to the summit. (While the gray slabs are fun, they lead to a false summit hundreds of yards east of the true summit.) Do not go straight up. Instead, stay left in the main gully as it works its way up to a point 200 feet left of the **summit** (4).

While the first half of the route climbs good rock, the second half has loose rock, and you should be very conscious of both your partner as well as any parties that may be below you.

An optional rack includes: 1 set of nuts and 1 ea .6-1" cams.

Retreat

Retreat the way you came up. Most people will feel comfortable downclimbing the route. However, if you are caught in a rainstorm, rappelling may be helpful and necessary for certain sections. There are no fixed anchors on the route so you will have to leave gear.

Chris McNamara

A view of the climbing route from the first red vein. The shattered red rock above is the routefinding crux— stay left as the arrow indicates. Do not climb straight up.

Third Pillar of Dana

From Mono Lake, the Third Pillar of the Dana Plateau (11,500') looks like a huge shark's tooth—the most prominent point on an escarpment of large cliffs. From the west, the Third Pillar is invisible until you are on top of it at the dramatic edge of an expansive plateau. The first sight when you get to the edge is of a steep, blocky, yet sheer pillar, and the skeptic expects any route that ascends such a steep final pitch to be 5.12. But only a few hours later, a stellar photograph of your partner will be had from the same point, on top of the pillar, victorious after some of the best (and most accessible) alpine climbing in the Sierra.

Approach

Park at the Tioga Lake Overlook (0.8 miles east of the Tioga Pass Entrance Station along Highway 120). Behind the bathrooms, find a wide fishermen's trail that leads down to the west end of Tioga Lake. Remain on the trail another 200 yards as it turns and parallels the south shore of Tioga Lake. When Glacier Creek meets Tioga Lake, leave the trail and walk cross-country following the east edge of the creek for a few hundred yards until a climbers' trail appears. This trail parallels the creek for about a mile

to Glacier Canyon—a long, shallow valley that rests between Mount Dana on the west and the Dana Plateau on the east. At this point, the well-defined climbers' trail ends. (From this point on there is a combination of climbers' trails and cross-country travel.) Continue on the trail for another 200 feet and gradually diagonal east up a rocky slope on a faint climbers' trail. After 200 yards, a second meadow is reached. Walk along the east end of the meadow for another few hundred yards until it is possible to head southeast up a large gully filled with orange talus (a distinct climbers' trail appears on the north edge of the gully after a few minutes). After a few hundred yards, a climbers' trail will traverse right and then disappear into a shallow, grassy valley in the middle of the Dana Plateau. Walk east up the shallow valley until you eventually reach a large field of 1- to 4-foot boulders. Walk east through the boulders all the way to the edge of the Dana Plateau. The striking prow of the Third Pillar of Dana will be visible 100 yards before you reach the dramatic edge of the plateau, and the top of the descent buttress is immediately to the west of the Third Pillar. Descend the buttress via low-angle 3rd class terrain; generally stay to the left, or 4th class drops must be negotiated. Cross the snow field to prominent ledges near the bottom of the snow chute, about 150 feet above the bottom of the rock on the Third Pillar.

bottom of the rock on the Third Pillar.

Descent

Reverse the approach.

Regular Route

approach

Chris McNamara

Regular Route 5.10b★★★★★

Time to climb route: **3-5 hours**

Approach time: **2-3 hours**

Descent time: **1-1.5 hours**

Sun exposure: **sunrise to noon**

Height of route: **600'**

This route has four pitches of three-star climbing leading to perhaps the most dramatic and highest quality single pitch in the High Sierra. The setting is much different than the Meadows: the climb is perched 5,000 vertical feet above Mono Lake with expansive high-desert scenery and 13,000-foot mountains in the distance. Every 5.10 Tuolumne climber should do this route.

FA: Phil Bircheff and Bill Bonebreak, 8/76.

Strategy

While the approach is relatively mild, the elevation coupled with the chance of afternoon thunderstorms dictate a dawn start. The Third Pillar is very popular and it is common to have more than one party on the route.

In early season (or all season in heavy snow years) there's a short snow slope just before the start of the climb. If you're careful and the snow is soft, you can usually kick steps in the snow with approach shoes. However, if the slope seems too steep or icy, continue downclimbing the 3rd class and cross once the snow gully is at a lower angle. An ice axe could be used but is rarely necessary unless the temperature is so low that climbing would not be enjoyable.

There is plenty of tricky routefinding and at least two variations to each pitch. While the route generally offers excellent protection, there is one short, scary face section. Right off a ledge mid-fourth pitch, a thin piton on the right protects tricky moves left into a small lieback flake. Although the moves are not too difficult once you commit, they look spooky and drive many climbers to attempt a bypass either to the left or the right. Both bypasses are dangerously runout and harder than they appear. Place protection on the ledge in case a fall pulls the piton and place RPs immediately below the piton.

The start of the last pitch allows a choice between dangerously loose flakes and a short, hard section of thin fingers below the left side of a roof. While many choose the flakes, protection would not likely hold and some sections are loose enough to rip off. As with any alpine climb, there is loose rock so wear a helmet.

Retreat

There are few fixed anchors so bring extra slings to leave on rock horns and chockstones (you may also have to leave nuts and cams). Only one rope is necessary for rappelling (if you made longer raps with two ropes they would likely get snagged).

The Dana Plateau is exposed to lightning danger, so check weather forecasts beforehand and retreat at the first sign of thunderstorm activity. Should you get caught in a serious thunderstorm on top, descend the 3rd class buttress to the bottom of the climb or lower and wait for the storm to dissipate, then re-ascend and hike out.

Regular Route		1	2	3	4	5
Free difficulty	≥5.10		●		●	●
	5.9	●				
	5.8			●		
	5.7					
	5.6					
	≤5.5					

Rack

nuts: 1 micro
　　　2 ea sml-med
　　　1 ea lrg
cams: 1 ea .4, 3"
　　　2 ea .5-2.5"
many slings

tons of steep,
flared grooves/cracks

sling
horn
1 150'
4th
3rd

5.8 finger

cool, big
detached flake

5.8
fist
5.9
arête
5.9
stem
160'

Normal
Start
3rd

traverse
snow gully

5.6 R
10"
8"
5.6 ow

5.8
flare
wide
crack

5.9
blocks
or
5.10b
roof

5.10a
stem
Direct
Start

120' 4 P

5.6
hand

5.10a R
1"
5.10b P
IRPs
5.11a R

5.10a
finger
5.8 flared squeeze
(3" in back)

detached flake

5.8 lb
.6-1.5"

belay takes
.6-1" and
sling flakes
160' 3

spectacular
belay location

5.6
chimney
enormous,
detached flake

5.8 fists

5.7
finger
5.8
pillar
bear-hug
thin
nuts
5.10a

5.7
flare
.75"

belay takes
1-3" 150' 2

5.7 ow

5.10a
flared
finger

5.9
hand

flared, steep
grooves

flake/
pillar

5.8
step
left
5.8
finger

1

5 130'

5.8 mantel

5.9
reach for
jugs or
mantel
5.9 hand

5.9 finger

5.10a lb
thin nuts

5.9 R
loose
flakes
5.10b finger
.4" cam

nuts, pins 4

Cathedral Peak

Cathedral Peak (10,911') is not only the most striking peak visible from Tuolumne Meadows, it is one of best 5.6 alpine rock climbs anywhere. Everything about the experience is incredible: the approach, the rock quality, the climbing, and, most of all, the summit. Not surprisingly this is also one of Tuolumne's most popular climbs, so be prepared to share the experience with others.

The letters above refer to the topo on page 117.

Approach

Park on the side of Highway 120 at the Cathedral Lakes trailhead. Follow the John Muir Trail for about 8 minutes. The trail will bend right, ascend 30 granite steps and then cut left. After 200 feet, find a well-traveled, 3-foot-wide, sandy climbers' trail that heads off left (about 15 feet before a stone runoff diverter and often blocked by logs so that hikers stay on the John Muir Trail). Follow this trail, most of which parallels Budd Creek, for about 45 minutes (1.5 miles) until the trail cuts right up a slope. The trail continues and gradually becomes more and more faint, at which point it's obvious how to walk cross-country up to the base of the Southeast Buttress.

Descent

From the summit, downclimb without a rope or downlead the final 20 feet. While this section is only 4th class, most will want a belay. The first climber should place pieces of pro intended to catch downward falls and clip them to the rope. Then the second will downclimb on lead, belayed by the first. You will be downclimbing the original line of ascent done by John Muir (without a rope and in heavy boots) in 1869.

From below the summit, move away from the climbing route on 3rd class. Once on a big ledge, traverse 15 feet down right, then down LEFT for 150 feet on 3rd class ledges, then work back right on 4th class ledges and slabs. From the base of the ledges and slabs, walk north to a ridge. Walk the ridge for 100 feet and then drop down (3rd class) to heavily used sandy trails and hike back down to the base. Walk out the way you came in.

The view of Cathedral Peak from the south side approach.

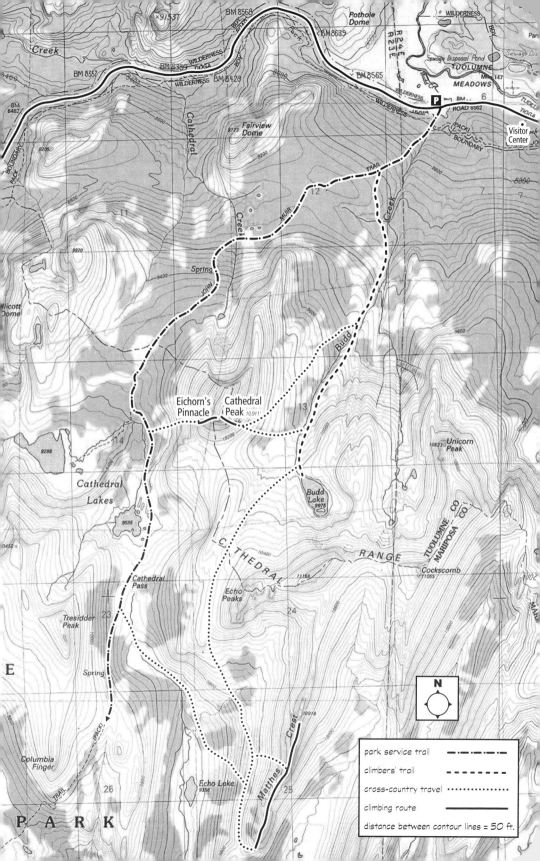

Southeast Buttress

5.6★★★★★

Time to climb route: **2-4 hours**

Approach time: **1.5 hours**

Descent time: **1.5-2 hours**

Sun exposure: **sunrise to afternoon**

Height of route: **700'**

Cathedral Peak is one of the most aesthetic routes in Tuolumne. The climb consists of five pitches of easy and moderate crack and face climbing in a perfect setting. The first few pitches are on low-angle terrain that gradually steepens and becomes more difficult. Because of its quality and moderate grade, this is one of the most crowded routes in Tuolumne. Luckily there are a number of variations if you need to pass a party.

FA: Chuck Wilts and Spencer Austin, mid-1940s.

History

John Muir didn't take long to seek out the most beautiful peak of the Tuolumne region. On his first trip to the Meadows, in 1869, he strolled up through virgin forests (no John Muir Trail then!) and scrambled to the top of what he named Cathedral Peak. The last bit was bona fide class 4, making it the hardest climb yet done in the country. Muir said afterwards, "This I may say is the first time I have been at church in California."

Muir, naturally, chose the easiest way, and his was the only route on the peak for the next 76 years. Along came Chuck Wilts, one of the Valley giants of the 1940s. An electrical engineer, Wilts was fortunate to spend the war years on Army/Navy rocket projects in Southern California. This meant that he was able to get away often to climb in the Sierra. His wife, Ellen, herself a brilliant climber, remembers his gear, ancient indeed by modern standards: "tennis shoes, hiking boots and even, on occasion, nailed boots. His clothing consisted of army-surplus full-cut climbing pants, a pullover parka, and a brimmed shade hat."

Wilts and Spencer Austin often climbed in the Valley on weekends in the early 1940s, and they were almost the only people in the Valley, with climbers and tourists alike involved in the war effort. Super climbers, they were the first to free the Regular Route on the Higher Cathedral Spire (1944). Later (1946 and 1947) they made valiant attempts on the Arrow Chimney, only to lose the route to John Salathé and Ax Nelson.

Virtually nothing is known about the history of the Wilts/Austin route on the Southeast Buttress of Cathedral Peak, even the year of the ascent. They never mentioned the climb in any major publication and, being modest men, never bragged about their soon-to-be classic route. The only clue—seven trivial words—appears in a mimeographed Sierra Club newsletter dated September 9, 1943, which states that in late July the pair "climbed the south side of Cathedral Peak." This could well have been the route we are talking about.

Whatever the year, it seems safe to say that they got the idea for their route by looking at that amazing profile of the buttress seen from many places along the Tioga Road east of the Meadows. It would be hard for a climber to scope that view and not want to be up there. Why no one had done the buttress in the 1930s is unclear, except that the pioneers back then usually sought out unclimbed summits rather than put up new routes.

Cathedral Peak	Pitch	1	2	3	4	5
Free difficulty	≥5.10					
	5.9					
	5.8					
	5.7					
	5.6		●	●	●	●
	≤5.5	●				

By the mid-1950s the route was a standard one, middling 5th class, and done by a few people on virtually every Sierra Club trip to Tuolumne. I did it when I was 16, in the company of an even-less experienced 17-year-old. We joyfully pounded our soft pitons into the decomposed cracks, taking hours (it seemed) to get them out, all twisted and scarred. Our excitement mounted as we got close to the top, manteling those big blocks of ultra-clean highcountry granite. On top of our first "big" climb, we realized we had become rockclimbers as well as mountaineers.

— Steve Roper

Strategy

There are no real routes up the Southeast Face, just an incredible sea of features that can be pieced together in an infinite number of variations. Because the face often has 10-15 people on it at a time, it's important to utilize these variations to avoid bottlenecks and slower parties. We highlight three main ways to climb the face, but you may create your own climb that combines pitches from all three. Route A gets most of the traffic, and although slightly easier, it is no more classic than Routes B and C. In fact, many pitches on Routes B and C are considered the best on the face.

To avoid crowds start early or, if you can climb fast, get a late start. Often if you start climbing before 8 a.m. or after 3 p.m. you will have most of the face to yourself. Because of the numerous climbers on the route, definitely wear a helmet and be careful of loose knobs and loose rock, especially 100 feet above The Chimney.

The summit is a 10,940-foot lightning rod and it's a miracle that no climbers have been killed by lightning. A climber was struck in summer 2000 and only luck and the Tuolumne SAR people were between him and the afterlife. Puffy clouds at the trailhead mean one thing: go climb something else!

For those who finish early, an amazing, improbable, and short 5.4 route will take you to the top of Eichorn's Pinnacle. Hopefully, you'll have a friend to take pics because the spectacular picture of you on top of Eichorn's Pinnacle, taken from the notch, is one to show off to family and friends. (See the SuperTopo for Eichorn's Pinnacle for more info, page 118.)

Before you start climbing, hang your backpack and any other gear in a tree as marmots will eat anything you leave at the base, including packs with no food.

Retreat

High Sierra thunderstorms and lightning sneak up on many Cathedral Peak climbers; be prepared in case you have to retreat. It is possible to retreat with just one 50m or 60m rope. However, two ropes will make retreat much faster and require leaving less gear. Many perfect nut placements and natural threads/horns mean that even a multi-pitch retreat will be reasonable. Of course, if a thunderstorm is on you just leave the dang cams and live to zap some food in a microwave, instead of learning what it feels like yourself!

To retreat from the base of The Chimney, walk right on the ledge, rappel off a slung flake (see topo, page 117) for two rappels with one 50m rope. If it's getting dark and you just need to get to the top quick, there are many spots on Pitches 4 and 5 where you can bail off left onto 4th and easy 5th class terrain.

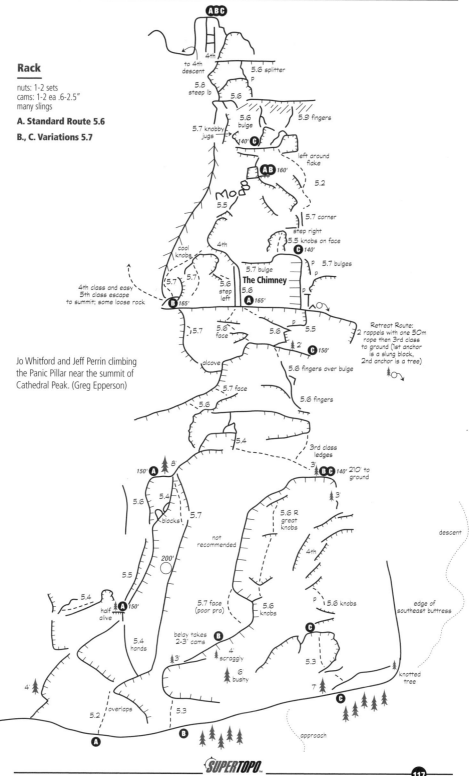

Rack

nuts: 1-2 sets
cams: 1-2 ea .6-2.5"
many slings

A. Standard Route 5.6

B., C. Variations 5.7

to 4th descent
4th
5.6 splitter
p
5.8 steep lb
5.6
5.6 bulge
5.9 fingers
5.7 knobby jugs
140' **C**
left around flake
A B 160'
5.2
Mod
5.5
5.7 corner
step right
5.5 knobs on face
cool knobs
4th
C 140'
5.7 bulge
p 5.7 bulges
p
The Chimney
5.7 5.7
5.6 step left
5.6
A 165'
p
4th class and easy
5th class escape
to summit; some loose rock
B 165'
5.7
5.6 face
5.6
5.5
p
Retreat Route:
2 rappels with one 50m
rope then 3rd class
to ground (1st anchor
is a slung block,
2nd anchor is a tree)
2'
C 150'
alcove
5.6 fingers over bulge

Jo Whitford and Jeff Perrin climbing
the Panic Pillar near the summit of
Cathedral Peak. (Greg Epperson)

5.7 face
5.6 fingers
5.6
5.4
3rd class ledges
150' **A** 8'
3'
B C 140' 210' to ground
3'
5.6
5.4
5.6 R great knobs
blocks
5.7
not recommended
4th
descent
200'
5.5
5.4 hands
5.4
half alive
A 150'
5.7 face (poor pro)
5.6 knobs
p 5.6 knobs
edge of southeast buttress
belay takes 2-3' cams
B
4' scraggly
C
5.3
3'
6' bushy
7'
knotted tree
4'
overlaps
5.3
C
5.2
A
B
approach

Eichorn's Pinnacle

Chris McNamara

One of the most spectacular spires of the Tuolumne region lies on the western flank of Cathedral Peak. Eichorn's Pinnacle, named after Jules Eichorn, one of the first ascensionists in 1931, must be the most photographed splinter of rock in Tuolumne. Seen from near the summit of the main peak, Eichorn's is beautifully outlined against Lower Cathedral Lake. It's worth doing just to get a picture!

– Steve Roper

Approach

West Pillar
Allow about 1.5 hours for the approach. Park on the side of Highway 120 at the Cathedral Lakes trailhead. Follow the John Muir Trail for about 2.5 miles and after a long, gradual climb switchbacking up a hill, the trail will head down a hill toward Cathedral Lakes. At this point, leave the trail to the left and walk cross-country to the base of the west face of Eichorn's Pinnacle. The route starts up the obvious wide crack.

Chris McNamara

North Face
Most climbers approach the North Face route by first climbing Cathedral Peak, then downclimbing and traversing 150 yards to Eichorn's Pinnacle. If not climbing Cathedral Peak, follow the approach for the West Pillar, but instead of walking to the base of the West Pillar stay to the left (north) and walk up 3rd class slabs to the notch between Eichorn's Pinnacle and Cathedral Peak.

Descent

A 70-foot rappel from the summit leads to 3rd class ledges. From here there are two descent options:

1) Scramble down 3rd class slabs back toward Cathedral Lake and the John Muir Trail.

2) Walk up a few hundred yards and pick up the descent for Cathedral Peak (see Cathedral Peak SuperTopo, page 112).

West Pillar 5.9★★★

Time to climb route: **2-4 hours**

Approach time: **1.5 hours**

Descent time: **1.5 hours**

Sun exposure: **noon to sunset**

Height of route: **700'**

A few hundred feet from the summit of Cathedral Peak stands Eichorn's Pinnacle—one of the most spectacular features in Tuolumne. While Cathedral Peak is an outstanding climb in its own right, combine it with Eichorn's Pinnacle and you will have ticked two of the most classic summits in Tuolumne.

The North Face, the most popular line, is one of the most exhilarating 5.4 climbs you will ever do. The West Pillar climbs five good pitches of sustained 5.8 and 5.9 (or a 5.10b variation) and joins up with the North Face before the summit.

FA: Gary Colliver and Mike Cohen, 7/72.
Variation: Alan Bartlett and Don Reid, 1979.

History

The North Face route was first climbed by Glen Dawson and Jules Eichorn on July 24, 1931. According to *Sierra Classics*, "As Eichorn and Dawson did not learn proper belay techniques until the next week at the Sierra Club's Underhill Camp, the ascent of Eichorn's Pinnacle was a daring adventure." In addition, the pair made the ascent without pitons and wearing tennis shoes. While this ascent was bold, a few years later Eichorn would make ascents of two far more dangerous and technical routes: Higher Cathedral Spire and Lower Cathedral Spire in Yosemite Valley.

The West Pillar of Eichorn's Pinnacle was first climbed in 1972 by Gary Colliver

West Pillar		1	2	3	4	5
Free difficulty	≥5.10					
	5.9	●	●			
	5.8			●		●
	5.7					
	5.6				●	
	≤5.5					

and Mike Cohen. On an attempt to repeat the original route in 1979, Don Reid and Alan Bartlett got off route and accidentally established the popular 5.10b variation.

– Chris McNamara

Strategy

There are rarely crowds on this climb. During Tuolumne's normally cool temperatures, it is better to start the climb after noon when the route goes into the sun. This route is well-protected even in the wide sections. There is no benefit to carrying a 60m rope.

Despite the ominous look of the wide first pitch, there are only a few short offwidth sections, and these can be stemmed around on knobs. After the first pitch there are two alternatives: the standard route traverses right, while the 5.10b variation continues straight up. The direct variation has some loose rock, but has better climbing than the 5.9 route.

For a great linkup, start the morning with Cathedral Peak, then descend the 3rd class slabs to the West Pillar of Eichorn's Pinnacle.

Retreat

It is possible to retreat with just one 50m rope, but you will have to leave gear. From the second belay on the standard route it's easy to bail off to the shoulder with one rappel and some downclimbing. From the top of the third pitch walk off on mellow 3rd and 4th class ledges.

A. North Face   5.4★★★★

FA: Glen Dawson and Jules Eichorn, 7/31.

This climb starts with a traverse off a large ledge onto tremendously exposed terrain. Though the moves are well-protected and rated 5.4, the exposure will get the blood pumping of even the most experienced climbers. The climb ends on a beautiful summit making a fantastic encore to climbing Cathedral Peak.

You may want to climb this route in two pitches to avoid rope drag. For a spectacular photo, have friends on the summit of Cathedral Peak take a shot of you while you stand on the summit of Eichorn's Pinnacle.

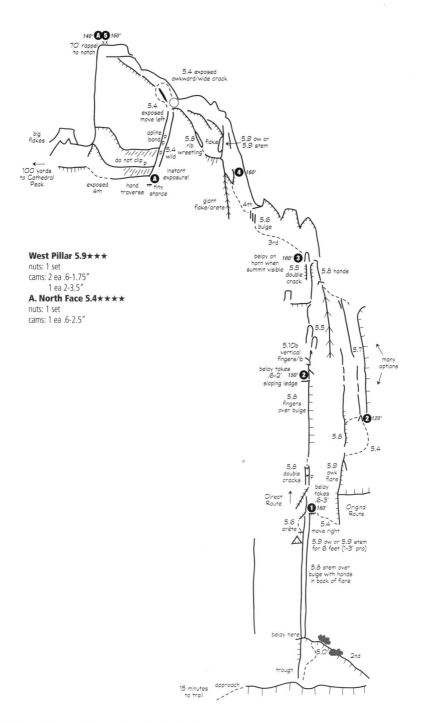

West Pillar 5.9★★★
nuts: 1 set
cams: 2 ea .6-1.75"
       1 ea 2-3.5"
A. North Face 5.4★★★★
nuts: 1 set
cams: 1 ea .6-2.5"

Brad Goya on the summit of Eichorn's Pinnacle. (John Brooks)

Matthes Crest

Matthes Crest is a true knife-edge ridge—a long fin of rock sculpted by glaciers. And unlike most such ridges, it is not a low point between peaks, but a completely independent formation. High and spectacular in a region of sweeping expanses of granite, Matthes Crest is unique.

Approach

Park on the side of Highway 120 at the Cathedral Lakes trailhead. Follow the John Muir Trail for about 8 minutes. The trail will bend right, ascend 30 granite steps and then cut left. After 200 feet, find a well traveled 3-foot-wide sandy climbers' trail that heads off left (about 15 feet before a stone runoff diverter and often blocked by logs so that hikers stay on the John Muir Trail). Follow this trail—most of which parallels Budd Creek—for about 1.5 miles to a creek crossing where a small trail heads up on the right bank of the creek. This is the Cathedral Peak climbers' trail. Instead of taking it, cross the logs and head up the main trail on the west side toward Budd Lake. From the west end of the lake head south and a little west contouring around the steep slopes of Echo Peaks. When Matthes Crest is visible, descend a little and walk cross-country for about 30 minutes to the south end.

Descent

Rappel off the North Summit, then either retrace your steps by the Echo Peaks or head west to the large meadow, join the John Muir Trail, and hike north along the western side of Cathedral Peak. While this second option looks attractive to those wary of the hike back up through the Echo Peaks, it is substantially longer in both distance and time.

Scott Justham finishing out the northern section of Matthes Crest. (Shawn Reeder)

Traverse from South to North 5.7★★★★★

Time to climb route: **3-6 hours**

Approach time: **2-3 hours**

Descent time: **2-3 hours**

Sun exposure: **sunrise to afternoon**

Height of route: **500' (length is 1 mile)**

Matthes Crest is sought after for its length, enjoyable climbing, and spectacular position in the midst of some of the most amazing scenery anywhere. This route climbs mostly 4th class on an exposed ridge with sections of technical climbing. Dozens of short routes have also been done on the sides of the Crest since the 1960s, but have generally not been recorded. Most parties only do two-thirds of the ridge—yet the climbing is great for the entire length.

FA: Chuck and Ellen Wilts, 1947.

History

No tourist has ever set eyes on Matthes Crest. A generalization, yes, but it depends on the definition of a tourist. Mine: One who goes through a national park quickly, never getting more than a few miles from the road. Matthes Crest, hidden away south of Tuolumne Meadows, is visible from no road and from no close trail. Only those who look directly south or directly north from close up will find this stupendous blade of granite worthy of attention. The writer and climber Michael Cohen has enjoyed a long love affair with the peak and recently wrote, "When you get up high, it sometimes appears as a striking, dramatic form blazing white in the sun, but on cloudy days Matthes Crest seems to fade into the bare bones of the region, being only one small part of a vast collection of exposed granite ribs that punctuate the domes and peaks of the Tuolumne region." Cohen also called the formation "a knife edge, a serrated white cleaver, great and wondrous." How true!

Once called Echo Crest, the blade attracted 1930s climbers looking for virgin summits. On July 26, 1931, Jules Eichorn, Walter Brem, and Glen Dawson made the first ascent. In their concise words, "We climbed the highest point from the east. It also looked possible from the west. The rock is weathered so as to be rotten and insecure. We found no record of former ascent."

Around 1949 the peak was christened after the Sierra's most eminent geologist, Dr. François Matthes, who had recently died. Wrote Reid Moran at the time, "He was the rare man of science who, through the clarity and simplicity of his prose, made his great knowledge of the geological story available not merely to his professional colleagues but also to the mountain-loving layman." Matthes wrote extensively about the Sierra and invented the term "cockscomb" to describe the rooster-comb-like formations that so dominate the mountains immediately south of Tuolumne Meadows.

Chuck Wilts (first free ascent of the Higher Cathedral Spire; first ascent of the Southeast Buttress of Cathedral Peak) made the first ascent of the now-classic south-to-north traverse in 1947 with his favorite climbing partner, his bride Ellen. Typical of the pair, they didn't bother to write anything about their route. For them, it was just another wonderful day in the mountains.

The route appeared in the first High Sierra guide, in 1954, but the description didn't much help. Here it is in full: "Ascend the south arête above a group of pines and traverse along the ridge." Even worse is the description from my 1972 guidebook: "The most pleasant route is a complete traverse of the ridge from south to north; this is 5.3 and a true classic." R. J. Secor's 1992 guidebook added more information—but it was still vague: "Four class 4-5 pitches lead to the top of the crest. Many spectacular and enjoyable class 3-4 pitches over slabs, pinnacles, and knife-edges lead to the base of the north peak." Secor rated the climb 5.6. My 5.3 rating came from the memory of a crazy cragrat who did the route unroped as a teenager. Me.

– Steve Roper

Strategy

Despite the long approach, Matthes often has a line. Luckily, it's usually easy to pass people. The climb is at least 18 pitches if you belay every pitch. Most parties, however, will only belay the handful of 5th class pitches and simul-climb or free solo the 3rd and 4th class sections. The climb can take as little as three hours if simul-climbed and over 12 hours if every pitch is belayed. Two ropes are needed for the descent if you stop after two-thirds of the ridge, making lightweight double ropes useful. Beware of loose rock, especially in the first few pitches.

Rappelling from the south summit is the most common mistake—it's unusual for the ropes not to get snagged. Instead, climb back down the ridgetop for 100 feet then traverse easy ledges on the east side of the ridge. Place pro to protect followers. Most parties rappel from the north summit (two double-length rappels to the west); continuing north presents increasing difficulties and great climbing but poor protection, especially for the follower.

The Matthes Crest is highly exposed and should not be attempted in any sort of inclement weather, especially during the common Sierra afternoon thunderstorms.

Slower parties should consider backpacking in and camping at Echo Lake to the west of Matthes Crest. A small number of overnight permits are available at the Tuolumne Meadows Wilderness Permit Center.

Retreat

It is possible to retreat off of the side of Matthes Crest by leaving slings and pro at almost any point. Care should be taken to avoid rope snags—multiple short rappels are better than long rappels. Rappelling the 600- to 800-foot-tall west face is usually the best course. Many parties have done this over the years, and routes up the side have also been done, so it is common to find old nuts, slings, and pitons—do not trust these alone!

The start of the Traverse from South to North.

Chris McNamara

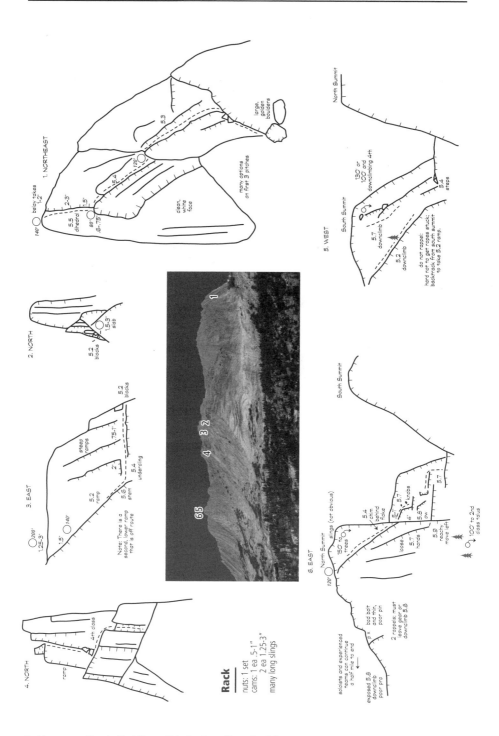

Brad Larson summiting the North Tower of Matthes Crest. (Shawn Reeder)

Rack

nuts: 1 set
cams: 1 ea .5-1"
      2 ea 1.25-3"
many long slings

Tenaya Peak

Tenaya Peak is unusual rock for Tuolumne—predominantly slick, cleanly fractured with no knobs—similar to the rock found right next to the car at the base of Stately Pleasure Dome. From the top, an amazing view is had of Half Dome to almost every spot in Tuolumne, with Mt. Conness in the distance, and Matthes Crest to the east.

Approach

Park at the large parking lot with bathrooms, about 300 yards northeast of Tenaya Lake. Hike straight across the woods and meadows, aiming for the toe of the buttress. Work up surprisingly good deer trails to the left, then scramble and bushwack a bit to reach the toe of the rock. If you get on the main lower ledge, a short polished scramble leads up a waterchute, or simply work back left and go up and around. In general, the scrambling is easier than it looks. Look for trails and paths around difficulties.

Descent

Hike west down the ridge from the summit, generally staying to the left side of the actual ridgetop. After about 0.5 miles, start looking for an open bouldery area about 200 yards below some large rock formations on the ridgetop. Work around to the right and join the main ledge system. It helps to have carefully eyed the ledge system from the car ahead of time. There are some hard climbs on steep cliffs above the ledge once you start down. Follow the ledge all the way back (but be very careful, it's easy to get on dirty steep slabs). Once back at the start of the ledge, descend back down where you came up (or thrash down almost anywhere).

An easier, but longer, alternative is to keep hiking down the ridge until you reach a major hiking trail, then follow this back to the right. When the trail splits, the left branch leads to the road at the Sunrise trailhead at the west end of the lake, and the right contours along the lake back to the beach. This latter trail is very beautiful, with perfect views of the lake and Stately Pleasure Dome on the far side.

Northwest Buttress

descent

Chris McNamara

Northwest Buttress 5.5★★★★

Time to climb route: **5-7 hours**

Approach time: **30 minutes**

Descent time: **1-1.5 hours**

Sun exposure: **afternoon to sunset**

Height of route: **1,500'**

This route looks loose and blocky, but in reality it climbs clean and amazing white granite. Unlike the knobby, flaky granite of Cathedral Peak and Matthes Crest, the granite here is slick and cleanly fractured. The crux moves are 5.5 friction and almost every pitch is 5.0-5.4—not 3rd or 4th class blocks like many other long, easier routes.

FA: Wayne Merry and John Ward, 7/61.

Strategy

Snow can be a problem on this route. Often a snow patch sits in the middle of the route until late June or July, and large slab avalanches have been seen in May. The snow condition is obvious from the road; if there's any snow on the buttress, wait until later in the season. The snow patch normally sits at the crux of the route, and to bypass it to the right will involve harder climbing on unknown terrain.

The route is popular but even if others are on it there are dozens of ways to pass slower parties during the first half of the route. Do not underestimate the length.The route appears foreshortened while you are on it—that tree that looks like it's one pitch up may well be four rope lengths ahead!

Getting to the start of the route is straight-forward until the last few hundred feet, where wet conditions, trees, loose rocks, and small cliffs must be negotiated. Unusually good trails, apparently from deer, are found in the lower brush.

There are a few options to finish the route: an easy traverse off left, a steep 5.8 hand crack or a loose, blocky finish up and right. If you feel comfortable dealing with loose rock, the right finish is the most direct and easiest route to the top, but the traverse off left is the standard finish. The 5.8 finish is fun, but somewhat grainy and mossy so it is not recommended unless you're comfortable at the grade.

Retreat

Since the route is longer than it looks and ascends a high point, watch out for storms. It's possible to retreat off left at many points in the first half of the route, but rappelling involves leaving a lot of gear. There are many old fixed pitons in the upper half of the route and a few trees, but again gear is likely needed for rappel stations. Two ropes are not mandatory for retreat, but allow more rappelling options.

Northwest Buttress	1	2	3	4	5	6	7	8	9	10	11	12	13	14
Free difficulty ≥5.10														
5.9														
5.8														
5.7														
5.6														
≤5.5	●	●	●	●	●	●	●	●	●	●	●	●	●	●

Rack

nuts: 1 set
cams: 2 ea .6-2"
     1 ea 3-4"

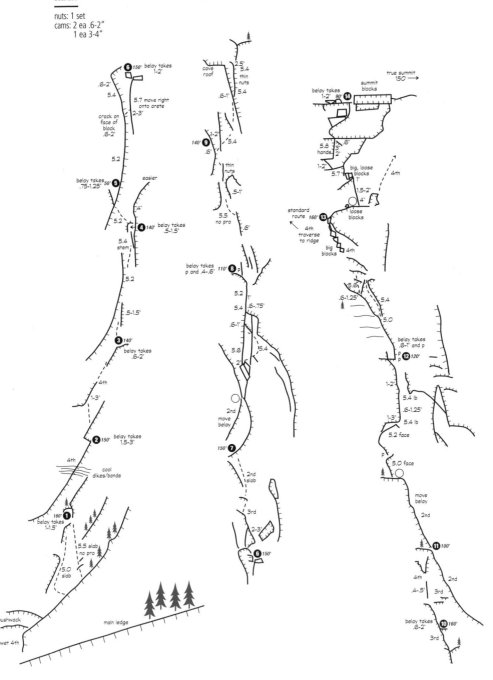

Barry Hutten enjoys the view from the summit of the West Ridge of Mt. Conness. (Greg Barnes)

Mt. Conness, North Ridge

The North Ridge (12,950') provides the perfect alpine experience without too many logistics. The approach passes streams, lakes, and a glacier, and the climb ascends an aesthetic, exposed ridge. You cover a variety of terrain from low-angle scrambling to steep downclimbing to exposed traversing—all on white granite.

Approach

The approach takes 2-3 hours, is about 4 miles long, and gains 1,700 feet in elevation. Of that, 1.7 miles are on hikers' trail and about 2.3 miles are on climbers' trail and cross-country. This is a relatively moderate and straightforward approach by High Sierra standards.

From Tioga Pass, drive east 2.2 miles on Highway 120 and turn onto the Saddlebag Lake Road just east of the Tioga Pass Resort. Follow this sometimes paved and sometimes dirt road 2.5 miles and park at the dam. (Remove all food and scented items or bears will trash your car.)

Hike north on the trail on the west shore of Saddleback Lake (or pay for a ferry crossing in the summer). After 1.3 miles, when the trail forks at a distinct boulder, go left and walk to the west end of Greenstone Lake where the trail fades. Cross the inlet of the lake and walk west, passing a sign that says "No camping or wood fires in Hall Natural Area." Follow a faint trail across a meadow until it gets more defined, starts trending right, and goes up a hill that parallels the creek. After a few hundred yards you reach a meadow and a waterfall. Scramble right of the waterfall on slabs and then trend left, above the waterfall, to Conness Lakes.

Stay on the right (north) shores of the Conness Lakes and at the last lake head up and skirt the right side of the talus. At the top of the talus, meet a wide 300-foot-tall cliff band right (northwest) of a moraine in front of the Conness Glacier (see photo below). Climb up sand and scree on the left-most manageable-looking gully (some 4th class) that is just right of where the cliff band becomes steep and 5th class. It's hard to see which gully to take—if the gully looks too steep then move right to another gully.

At the top of the gully, traverse left above the cliff band staying just above the bushes. Continue traversing until you gain the ridge just above a col and the start of the North Ridge. Walk on the ridge for a few hundred yards as the ridge transitions from 2nd to 3rd class. When the ridge steepens to 4th class, rope up and start climbing.

Descent

The West Ridge and the North Ridge share the same descent, which is also the approach for the West Ridge. From the summit, go down the 2nd class southeast ridge trail to the large sandy plateau. Walk to the northeast corner of the plateau. (Don't lose elevation when traversing the plateau even if other trails go down.)

4th class

Chris McNamara

Drop down the East Ridge and head a little right (south) to a flat section. Continue east and find a way down a cliffy section and then aim for the bottom of the valley. Eventually you'll reach a faint trail that gradually gets more pronounced until it turns into a major trail. Pass the Carnegie Institute and continue east past the Sawmill Campground to the road. Walk up the road about 0.5 mile to Saddlebag Lake and your car.

Approach GPS Coordinates

Parking area at Saddlebag Lake dam:
    37° 57' 885", 119° 16' 367"
Split in trail at distinct boulder:
    37° 58' 708", 119° 17' 567"
Inlet of Gemstone Lake:
    37° 58' 676", 119° 17' 564"
Just before waterfall below Conness Lakes:
    37° 58' 810", 119° 17' 877"
150 yards above last Conness Lake:
    37° 58' 523", 119° 18' 813"
Col at the start of the North Ridge:
    37° 58' 471", 119° 19' 143"
Summit of Mt. Conness:
    37° 58' 014", 119° 19' 278"

A view of the crux downclimb from below.

North Ridge 5.6★★★★

Time to climb route:	**3-8 hours**
Approach time:	**2-3 hours**
Descent time:	**2-3 hours**
Sun exposure:	**partial sun to shade**
Height of route:	**800'**

This great introduction to alpine rock climbing ascends long stretches of 3rd and 4th class occasionally interrupted with an exposed 5.6 move. Even the 3rd class sections are interesting and fun. You choose the exposure and climbing difficulty by either staying directly on the ridge (harder) or moving to either side of the ridge (easier). Following the climbing route is straightforward, but the approach and descent are more devious and require skill using a USGS map. Located at a relatively low elevation, this climb is usually warm enough to climb up until the first snow of the year (usually in November). Compared with Cathedral Peak, the North Ridge has less technical climbing but much more hiking, routefinding, and elevation gain.

FA: Galen Rowell and Barry Hagen, 1969.

Strategy

It's best to climb the route car-to-car in a day. Because the descent doesn't pass by where you would camp at Conness Lakes, bivying on the approach means hiking back at least 4 miles round-trip to recover your gear after the climb.

Most climbers need a full day for the climb and should start at dawn. The first half of the climb receives sun in the morning and the second half gets sun in the afternoon. The climbing can be quite cold in the shade so bring gloves and warm clothes. The time to climb the route will vary from 3-8 hours depending on how many sections you rope up for. If you plan to rope up for much of the climb, get a pre-dawn start. The route is relatively popular

but there are many ways to pass other climbers. For a rack, bring a lightweight lead line and a small selection of nuts and cams. Many climbers free solo the route except for the 5.6 downclimb, which is rappelled with one 120-foot-long rope.

Route description

From the col at the beginning of the North Ridge, walk a few hundred yards until the ridge steepens. Rope up when necessary. Climb about 300-400 feet (two roped pitches) of 3rd then 4th class until the ridge flattens. Walk for a few hundred feet to just below First Tower, which has a distinct visor. Traverse under First Tower staying on the east side of the ridge on exposed 3rd class. Downclimb into a notch then climb up a few hundred feet of 3rd and occasionally 4th class to the top of Second Tower. Stop here for a snack, take in the view, and prepare for the crux downclimb.

The crux starts just below Second Tower by either rappelling 30 feet from slings or downclimbing 5.5 to a second set of slings. From here, either rappel 60 feet or downclimb a big 5.6 corner. After the downclimb/rappel, ascend 500 feet of sustained 4th class with the occasional 5th class move. For the best and most exhilarating climbing, stay near but not on the ridge. When the ridge flattens out, walk a few hundred feet to the summit.

For super fast and motivated climbers, consider climbing the West Ridge before or after the North Ridge.

Retreat

Carry one 50m or 60m rope to retreat. From before Second Tower, reverse the route, which will either require downclimbing or rappelling and leaving gear (there are few fixed anchors). From after Second Tower, the easiest option is to finish climbing the route. If you are caught near the summit and must bivy or take cover, there are some stonewall bivy spots southwest of the summit.

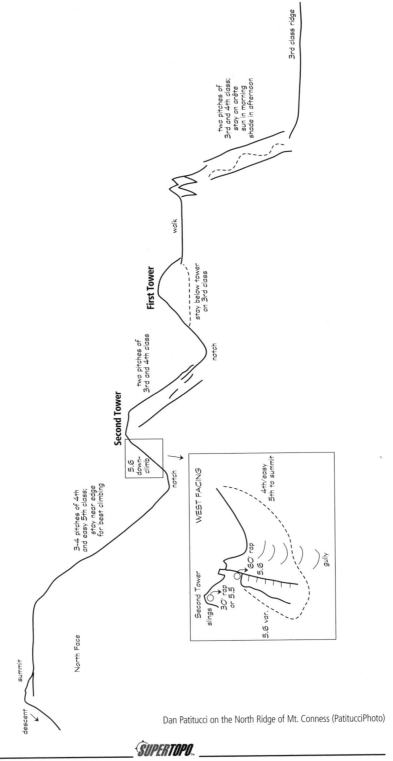

Dan Patitucci on the North Ridge of Mt. Conness (PatitucciPhoto)

Labels within diagram:

3rd class ridge

two pitches of
3rd and 4th class;
stay on arête
sun in morning
shade in afternoon

walk

First Tower

stay below tower
on 3rd class

notch

two pitches of
3rd and 4th class

Second Tower

5.6 down-climb

notch

3-4 pitches of 4th
and easy 5th class;
stay near edge
for best climbing

North Face

summit

descent

WEST FACING

4th/easy
5th to summit

Second Tower

slings

30' rap
or 5.5

60' rap
5.6

gully

5.6 var.

Mt. Conness, West Ridge & Southwest Face

Unlike most Sierra peaks, which gently rise on the western slopes and drop-off to the east, Mt. Conness (12,590') is dominated by a 1,200-foot southwest face. The wall is so impressive it's easy to overlook the gentle sweep of the West Ridge on the left. This once obscure feature has been rediscovered in the last ten years as maybe the best 5.6 ridge in the Sierra.

Approach

The approach takes 3-6 hours, is about 4.5 miles long, and gains 2,500 feet in elevation before losing about 800 feet. Of that, one mile is on hikers' trail and about 3.5 miles is on climbers' trail and cross-country. This is a strenuous and confusing approach. Do it with someone who has done it before and give yourself plenty of time.

Take the Saddlebag Lake Road off of Highway 120, 2.2 miles outside the East Entrance to the park, just below the Tioga Pass Resort, and about 0.5 mile above Ellery Lake. Follow the sometimes paved and sometimes dirt road for 1.6 miles and park in the Sawmill Campground parking area on the left. If you reach Saddlebag Lake, you have gone too far.

Follow the dirt road to the campground. This dirt road eventually passes the Carnegie Institute (just a dilapidated wooden shed). Soon after that, the road turns to well-established trail and then a faint trail.

The GPS coordinate for one place to leave the trail is 37° 57' 632", 119° 17' 361". However, you can leave the trail at almost any point when about 5-10 minutes past the Carnegie Institute.

Here the approach turns to cross-country travel, so orient yourself to the USGS map. Travel northwest aiming for a brushy gully in a cliffy section (a climbers' trail goes through the cliffy section).

At the top of this, the terrain flattens (a good place to camp) and you pass a few smaller lakes (dry in late season). Continue up a mostly grassy hillside to another flat area with a lake (last water source). Continue up toward the East Ridge. A final section of sandy 2nd and 3rd class scrambling puts you on the expansive sandy plateau that leads to the clearly visible summit of Mt. Conness.

West Ridge

Southwest Face

Greg Barnes

Stash a water bottle here along with anything else you don't want to take on the climb. Beware that marmots will eat any food you leave.

Next, head west and down the sandy slope dropping 100-200 feet in elevation. Aim for the most distinct notch across the plateau (Do not go down the notch just below the summit!)

There are a few notches to choose from, most of which cliff out. Only go down the notch from which you can see the entire southwest face from summit to base.

approach

Carnegie Institute

Chris McNamara

Head straight down the gully for several hundred yards, following sandy, loose, and steep 2nd and 3rd class trails. When you encounter a steep section, stay to the left. Once past the steep section, some scree leads to talus. From here, follow the description for the route you are climbing.

For the West Ridge continue down staying about 300 feet away from the southwest face. The West Ridge starts just left of the obvious toe of the buttress. There are two arêtes separated by a gully. The route starts on the left arête.

For the Southwest Face, aim for the left side of the steep part of the face. The route starts about 80 feet left of a plaque in memory of Don Goodrich who was killed on the face. The route starts in grassy cracks (usually wet) to the right of a series of tiered roofs and right-facing corners.

Alternate Approach

The following approach is longer than the above but more straightforward. It is best suited for climbers who want to avoid the tricky routefinding of the standard approach and don't mind adding an extra day or two to the climb. Get a Wilderness Permit in Tuolumne, park at Lembert Dome, and backpack into the Young Lakes or a bit beyond (consult the permit rangers). Camp at Young Lakes. Climb the next day with the lightest, smallest pack possible. Enjoy the far more leisurely pace required to do the route and for fun, pick the best-looking line on the upper pitches, avoiding the easier 4th class in favor of endless easy 5th class. This approach is too long for a one day car-to-car climb.

Descent

The West Ridge, Southwest Face, and the North Ridge share the same descent, which is also the approach for the West Ridge and Southwest Face. From the summit, go down the 2nd class southeast ridge trail to the large, sandy plateau. Walk to the northeast corner of the plateau. Don't lose elevation when traversing the plateau even if other trails go down. From here, reverse the approach.

Backcountry Camping

While it is common to climb Conness car-to-car in a day, this makes for a demanding day. There are two options for camping on the approach: Young Lakes (if coming from Tuolumne Meadows), and Alpine Lake (if coming from Sawmill Campground). The approach to Young Lakes is longer but rewards you with a great view of the route. For either option you need a backcountry permit, available in Tuolumne Meadows.

West Ridge 5.6★★★★★

Time to climb route: **3-6 hours**

Approach time: **3-5 hours**

Descent time: **2-3 hours**

Sun exposure: **noon to sunset**

Height of route: **1,500'**

The West Ridge of Mt. Conness is perhaps the best moderate alpine climb in Tuolumne. With the competition including Cathedral Peak and Matthes Crest, this says a lot. TM Herbert described it as "great fun, like two Cathedral Peaks stacked on top of each other." Peter Croft called it the best route he had done in the Sierra backcountry (albeit before embarking on some of his recent mega-traverse link-ups). Those familiar with the numerous options climbers encounter on Cathedral and Matthes will be overwhelmed with Mt. Conness—there are hundreds of possible starting points, and nearly every pitch has dozens of possible variations.

The West Ridge is an indistinct line with many options, and several veteran climbers have said that the most classic option starts a hundred yards down and left of the topo route on the ridge edge/arête to the left. Many options are available and all are fun, so don't limit your options, especially if other parties are ahead. The ridge is clean, but the farther you stray from the true ridge, the more loose rock you will find.

FA: Dick Long, Jim Wilson, 1957.

History

Starting in the summer of 1957, a variety of technical climbers started basing at Tuolumne Meadows, and the most impressive possibility in range from there was the southwest face of Mt. Conness. Career-long partners Dick Long and Jim Wilson were among those who went up to look at the wall, but they were alpine climbers (who in 1965 would pioneer the biggest route in North America, Mt. Logan's Hummingbird Ridge), not wall climbers, and they turned away. Soon afterward, however, they had to go back to the base to help in the grim task of evacuating the body of Don Goodrich, who had died when he pulled off a loose block.

Within a week or two, Long and Wilson came back to climb what had looked like a reasonable and enjoyable route on the wall's west flank. They started hiking from Tuolumne early in the morning and when they got to Conness their view confirmed that the cracks and exfoliations along the crest above the southwest face looked like an enjoyable climb. Long remembers the climbing as "pure joy," and they placed only one piton the whole way, at the crux about two-thirds of the way up. They finished the route with no idea that they had done a first ascent. Night fell during the long hike back, and it was nearly 4 a.m. before they made it back to the road.

The route fell into obscurity until the late 1980s, when Peter Croft started visiting the area. In his search for quality, not difficulty, he came back from this route, as he would from many others, raving that Conness' west ridge "is one of the best routes in the High Sierra."

– Andy Selters

West Ridge		Pitch 1	2	3	4	5	6	7	8	9	10	11	12
Free difficulty	≥5.10												
	5.9												
	5.8												
	5.7												
	5.6	●	●										
	≤5.5			●	●	●	●	●	●	●	●	●	●

Strategy

Like many alpine climbs, the West Ridge of Conness must be climbed swiftly to be done in one day. Slower climbers, or those simply out to enjoy a beautiful backpack in the Sierra, should consider backpacking into the Young Lakes from Tuolumne. Due consideration for the availability of wilderness permits should be taken—don't expect to get one without planning in advance.

The weather on Mt. Conness can be more severe than surrounding areas due to the height and the sheer southwest face. Winds can be tremendous and lightning danger is extreme. Do not attempt this climb if thunderstorms are expected or if any clouds are seen.

Much of the approach is loose and sandy 2nd/3rd class. In early season snow and boggy conditions should be expected and footwear should reflect this. Even in late season, a pair of light gaiters will help keep sand out of your boots.

Retreat

Retreat is not recommended due to the high probability of rope snags and pulling rocks onto your head. If retreat is required, try to avoid the gully or anything that could snag the rope. Perhaps traverse a distance for each rappel to be sure that falling rock will not hit you. Gear must be left to retreat.

Do not get on this climb if there is any possibility of a storm.

Craig Adkins

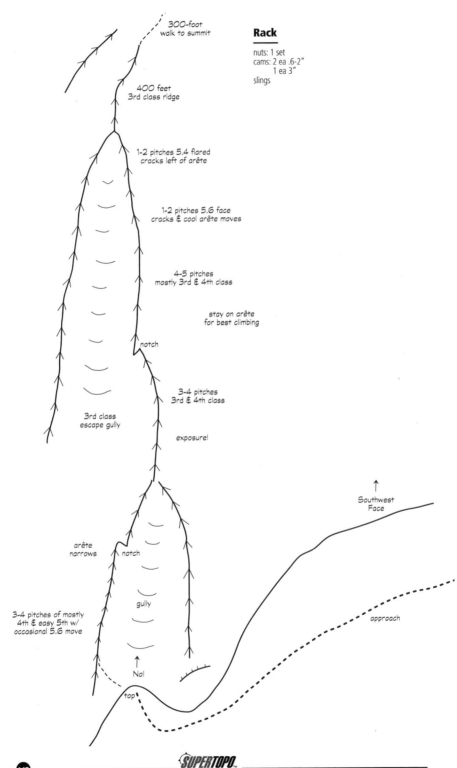

300-foot
walk to summit

Rack

nuts: 1 set
cams: 2 ea .6-2"
       1 ea 3"
slings

400 feet
3rd class ridge

1-2 pitches 5.4 flared
cracks left of arête

1-2 pitches 5.6 face
cracks & cool arête moves

4-5 pitches
mostly 3rd & 4th class

stay on arête
for best climbing

notch

3-4 pitches
3rd & 4th class

3rd class
escape gully

exposure!

Southwest
Face

arête
narrows   notch

gully

3-4 pitches of mostly
4th & easy 5th w/
occasional 5.6 move

approach

No!

top

Southwest Face 5.10c★★★★

Time to climb route:	**6-9 hours**
Approach time:	**3-5 hours**
Descent time:	**2-3 hours**
Sun exposure:	**all day**
Height of route:	**1,200′**

The sheer 1,200-foot white Southwest Face is the most prominent and alluring face in the Tuolumne area. If you climb 5.10 and you see it enough times, (and you will, since it is visible from Half Dome, Cathedral Peak and anywhere in between), you will eventually need to climb it. Standing at the base, the route looks impressive and intimidating with a big roof and steep corner looming midway up. Stout, wild, and exposed climbing is mixed in with lower angle moves. You must be in good offwidth shape for the sustained crux 5.10 wide pitch. The offwidth makes this climb just a touch harder than the Incredible Hulk's Red Dihedral. This route will help you get in shape for Keeler Needle. This route has one of the more incredible views of any Sierra peak: You look across Tuolumne Meadows, Grand Canyon of Tuolumne, Half Dome, Fairview Dome, and Cathedral Peak.

FA: Warren Harding, Glen Denny, Herb Swedlund, 9/59.
FFA: Galen Rowell, Chris Vandiver, 7/76.

History

When Warren Harding and his crew completed The Nose of El Capitan in November of 1958, Yosemite climbers started asking, "What's next?" One obvious answer was to take the methods of El Cap success to other walls, including the Sierra high country. Wally Reed was one

of Harding's stronger El Cap partners, and during the long months of Park Service enforced interims on Nose work in 1958, Reed was the first to look carefully for the possibilities for new walls around Tuolumne Meadows. He and Chuck Pratt came back from the first ascent of Fairview Dome in August of 1958, and their news of superb rock probably added to the impetus to check out the big face that a variety of wandering climbers had seen north of Tuolumne, the southwest face of Mt. Conness.

Early the next season, Don Goodrich organized a team to try this face. Just a few weeks before he had pioneered a classic new route to the top of a slab lying against the Glacier Point Apron. On Conness, just 150 feet up, Goodrich pulled on a block that came off; he fell with it and was killed.

Goodrich was well-liked, and the tragedy traumatized the Yosemite climbers. Soon though, they built a determination that an ascent of the wall in his name would be a fitting memorial. By September, Warren Harding collected a pair of relative newcomers: Herb Swedlund, a wiry man who would pioneer some great new routes in the Tetons in subsequent years; and Glen Denny, a tall, redheaded employee at Yosemite Lodge who had started climbing with Harding a year before on Washington Column.

Conness's face suggested that Goodrich's route choice had been a good one, but there was a short, loose section where he simply had met some very bad luck. His blood still discolored the rock, and as Swedlund led past the dark stain his head spun and his stomach turned. He finished the pitch but announced that his energy for leading had withered. He would haul as Harding and Denny led, and, in classic Harding style they took their time and enjoyed the struggles of nailing pins and jamming cracks and hauling gear. After a night on a ledge they worked up a chimney that led to a wide crack. Harding, an innovator at improvising wide pitons, hadn't packed much big iron to this backcountry wall, and so they drilled

Southwest Face	Pitch	1	2	3	4	5	6	7	8	9
Free difficulty	≥5.10		●		●	●				
	5.9	●					●	●		●
	5.8			●					●	
	5.7									
	5.6									
	≤5.5									

protection bolts to the right of the worst offwidth section. This took up enough time that they spent a second night on the wall, enjoying the wine that Harding always brought along. After a (probably hanging) bivouac higher up, they finished the route.

A few years later, Galen Rowell found some of his profound inspiration while climbing with Harding, and by the mid-1970s Rowell was aiming for technical routes in the Himalaya. He decided that Sierra winter ascents would be good preparation, and in February of 1976 he came to this face on Conness, with Dennis Hennek and Mike Graber. In full winter regalia it took them an afternoon to fix a couple of pitches, then a full day of aid and booted freeclimbing to reach an alcove where they hung in hammocks, waiting a cold night a couple of pitches below the top.

Four months later, Rowell hiked back in with Chris Vandiver, who figured he could make the first free ascent of the route. Starting the crux second pitch, Vandiver tried to climb directly upward. He couldn't work in any reliable protection, so he shifted to a tenuous rightward traverse. After struggling to get in a series of hexes and pitons in a flared horizontal crack, he committed to some desperate and scary moves, clipping his haul line into one piece so that Rowell could give him a two-rope belay. He panted and pulled an overhang, and found one foothold to pause on before working back toward the original route. A couple of more moves of 5.11 got him to easier terrain.They rappelled to the ground, leaving two ropes to ease their way to the first free ascent the next day.

– Andy Selters

Strategy

Many climbers do this route car-to-car in a day. However, to ensure success, you might consider camping somewhere on the approach or at Young Lakes. Despite the high elevation, temperatures can be scorching because the route faces south and is wind-sheltered. Bring plenty of water and wear versatile clothing so you can adjust your layers as the temperatures change. This is a great climb to do in late season when other climbs are too cold. A 60m rope allows you to link many pitches but is not mandatory.

The first pitch is the worst on the climb and can feel like 5.9 if dry and 5.10c if wet (it's usually wet). The second pitch starts with tricky routefinding: don't be suckered by the beautiful right-leaning crack. The second part of the second pitch is the technical crux of the route, but the business is the offwidth crux on the fourth pitch. This pitch has a few 5.10 moves between long stretches of 5.8 and 5.9 offwidth and chimney. A 7" cam might protect the crux (Big Bros certainly will). Otherwise you rely on a handful of ancient bolts for protection.

The next pitch has the exposure crux of the route where you must make a somewhat devious 5.10 face move right. You can link this pitch with the next in order to bypass a cramped belay, but beware of bad rope drag. The next few pitches are pretty straightforward with many belay options.

Retreat

It's possible to retreat with one 60m rope, but you will have more options and leave less gear with two ropes. There are some retreat stations just right of the route for the first few pitches. After that you must leave gear in order to retreat.

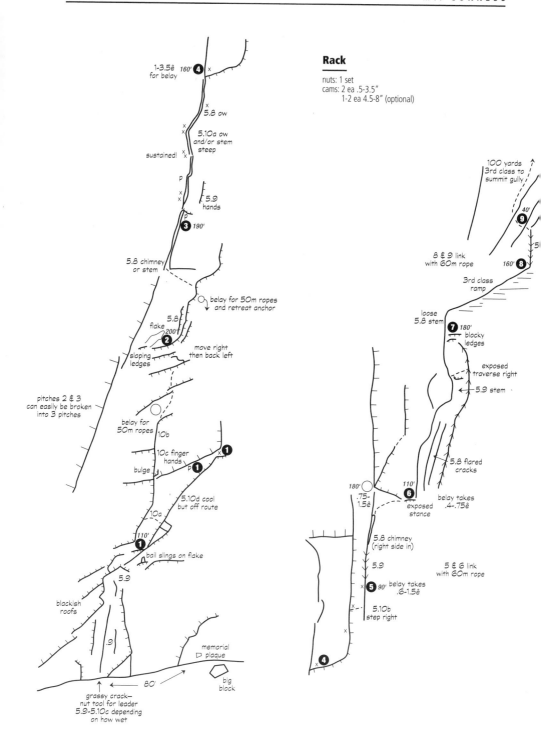

Rack

nuts: 1 set
cams: 2 ea .5-3.5"
       1-2 ea 4.5-8" (optional)

1-3.5ê 160' **4** x
for belay

x
5.8 ow

x
x
5.10a ow
and/or stem
steep
sustained! x x

p
x
x   5.9
hands

p
3 190'

5.8 chimney
or stem

belay for 50m ropes
and retreat anchor

5.8
flake 200'
2

move right
then back left

sloping
ledges

pitches 2 & 3
can easily be broken
into 3 pitches

belay for
50m ropes 10b

10c finger
hands
1
bulge p **1**

5.10d cool
but off route

10a

110'
1

bail slings on flake

5.9

blackish
roofs

.9

memorial
□ plaque

80'

big
block

grassy crack—
nut tool for leader
5.9-5.10c depending
on how wet

100 yards
3rd class to
summit gully

40'
9

5

8 & 9 link
with 60m rope 160' **8**

3rd class
ramp

loose
5.8 stem **7** 180'
blocky
ledges

exposed
traverse right

5.9 stem

5.8 flared
cracks

180' O
.75-
1.5ê
110'
6
exposed
stance

belay takes
.4-.75ê

5.8 chimney
(right side in)

5.9

5 & 6 link
with 60m rope

x **5** 90' belay takes
.6-1.5ê

x 5.10b
step right

x

4
x

Matterhorn Peak

Brad Goya

When driving U.S. 395 near Bridgeport, the jagged peaks of the aptly named Sawtooth Range dominate the skyline. Of these alluring summits, Matterhorn Peak (12,264') stands out because of its perfect symmetry, seemingly sheer face, and needle-point summit. While impressive, Matterhorn Peak bears little resemblance to its namesake of the Swiss Alps. While the climbing is only okay, this peak is popular due to its beauty and inclusion in Jack Kerouak's beat classic *Dharma Bums*. There is also something intriguing about this and any big peak visible from the road. See a beautiful peak enough times from the window of your car and it's hard to resist climbing it.

Approach

The trailhead for Matterhorn Peak is at Twin Lakes, 13 miles west of the town of Bridgeport. Take U.S. 395 to the north end of Bridgeport, turn west onto the Twin Lakes Road, and drive to its end in the Mono Village at the west end of the lake. There is a $5 parking fee.

This is a HUGE approach that starts out pleasant and gradually gets steeper, more difficult, and less fun. The approach takes most climbers 4-7 hours from Twin Lakes to the base of the climb and involves 2 miles on the main trail, 4 miles on climbers' trails and cross-country travel, and gains about 4,500 feet in elevation.

Finding the start of the trail is a little difficult. From the backpackers' parking, walk to the southeast corner of the RV campground where a wide wooden bridge crosses a creek. Continue south and a little east on unmarked trails over a few more creeks until you hit the big information board at the start of the Horse Creek Trail. Follow this trail for 2 miles until it forks. Stay right on what becomes an unmaintained but good climbers'/fishermen's trail that follows Horse Creek. For the next few miles the trail is usually obvious over mostly flat terrain but

sometimes travels through dense brush and over talus. In general, you stay within 100 feet of the left bank of Horse Creek.

Toward the end of the canyon you will contemplate crossing to the right side of the creek and heading up a gully. Don't do this. Instead, stay on the left side of the creek. Eventually the trail passes through red talus and begins to switchback up toward a col staying just left of some brush. Follow the edge of the brush and eventually traverse above the top of the brush (over water running through the talus) and follow a sometimes hard to see climbers' trail up a gully on red rock and dirt. The climbers' trail continues all the way up to a col.

Here there are many options, but generally you head cross-country southwest up a broad ridgeline. You will eventually reach a picturesque small and shallow alpine lake and meadow with a great view of Matterhorn Peak. If camping, stop here.

From here, you generally stay on the left side of the valley mostly on cross-country. As you near the face, you have to deal with more talus, scree, and snow. Eventually you reach the glacier and steep scree leading to the base of the north arête. The route starts a few hundred feet up and left from the toe of the arête.

Descent

From the summit, walk east to the gully. A scree climbers' trail leads back to the start of the route. From here, reverse the approach.

Backcountry Camping

Only exceptionally fit and fast climbers do this route car-to-car in a day. Most people take two days. On the first day, hike to the alpine lake described above at 9,800 feet. Wake up early, climb the route in the morning and then hike out in the afternoon. This is a spot worth hanging out at. Above the meadow and small lake rise massive peaks, moraine, and talus. Below, the topography falls away for an expansive view of Horse Creek Canyon. If you camp, even if you don't climb the peak, you'll enjoy the pristine wilderness setting.

Chris McNamara

GPS Coordinates

Red rock above bushes:
   38° 06' 732", 119° 22' 424"
Top of col: 38° 06' 539", 119° 22' 294"
Alpine Lake bivy:
   38° 06' 430", 119° 22' 563"
Ridge, left side of canyon:
   38° 06' 315", 119° 22' 549"
Start of talus: 38° 06' 152", 119° 22' 614"
Base of route: 38° 06' 646", 119° 22' 877"

See USGS map for Incredible Hulk on page 153.

Chris McNamara

"What does he care if he hasn't got any money: he doesn't need any money, all he needs is his rucksack with those little plastic bags of dried food and a good pair of shoes and off he goes and enjoys the privileges of a millionaire in surroundings like this."

– Jack Kerouac

North Arête 5.7★★★

Time to climb route: **3-6 hours**

Approach time: **4-7 hours**

Descent time: **4-7 hours**

Sun exposure: **sunrise to noon**

Height of route: **700'**

The North Arête offers relatively moderate and adventurous climbing for those who don't mind a massive approach. After a few pitches of loose rock, the climbing is pretty good for four pitches. It's not the best climbing in the High Sierra, but appeals because it is not too difficult and ascends a striking arête on a big and aesthetic peak. It's one of the easier climbs that gives a complete alpine rock experience: a glacier, striking summit, incredible views—all at high-elevation. After the first few unpleasant pitches, the routefinding eases and the rock quality gets better and better. This route is a slight step up in difficulty from the East Face of Mt. Whitney.

FA: Jerry Gallwas, Wally Kodis, Don Wilson, 9/54.

History

This route was first done by two of the great pioneers of modern American rockclimbing. Don Wilson and Jerry Gallwas were Sierra Club partners who were at the core of southern California's rockclimbing revolution, focused on Tahquitz Rock. In 1952, Wilson and Royal Robbins invented the "decimal" gradations for 5th class climbing, giving us our legacy of "5.5, 5.8" etc. Gallwas was a favored partner because he made some of the finest pitons around. He took Chuck Wilts' knifeblade idea of using chrome-moly aircraft steel to make angles and beefy horizontals. In the summer of 1954,

Wilson and Gallwas individually made a couple of the first close inspections of the great northwest face of Half Dome. A year later they joined with Robbins and Warren Harding to make the first serious attempt, and in 1957 Gallwas, Robbins, and Mike Sherrick made the wall's first ascent.

The north arête of Matterhorn Peak was a much more recreational objective, and Wilson, Gallwas, and Wally Kodis climbed it in September of 1954, soon after those first probes on Half Dome. They took a 4th class ledge to access the arête partway up. A variety of teams later started by climbing the lower buttress; the most direct way was first done in 1974 by Bruce McCubbrey and Ruprecht Kammerlander, a touring climber who three years later would make an impressive speed ascent of Denali's west rib—alone.

– Andy Selters

Strategy

Start early and move fast so you can climb this route in the sun. The route gets cold when it goes into the shade, especially when the often icy afternoon winds kick up. A 50m rope works just as well as a 60m rope. Wear a helmet and watch for loose rock if there are climbers above or below you.

The start of the route is indistinct and hard to find. Begin a few hundred feet up and left from the bottom of the face/arête. Look for the easiest loose ramp system that angles up and right to the arête. Once on the arête, you wander back and forth staying as close as you can to the arête until harder moves occasionally force you right. A few hundred feet from the top, move to the left side of the arête. The crux last pitch fortunately has the best rock on the route. Carry 3.5-4.5" cams to protect this section, or if you don't want carry the weight of big gear on this climb, just run it out.

Retreat

There are no fixed anchors on this route so you must leave gear in order to retreat. Having a second retreat rope does not help much since longer rappels just mean the rope is more likely to snag.

		Pitch					
North Arête		1	2	3	4	5	6
Free difficulty	≥5.10						
	5.9						
	5.8						
	5.7						●
	5.6	●				●	●
	≤5.5		●	●			

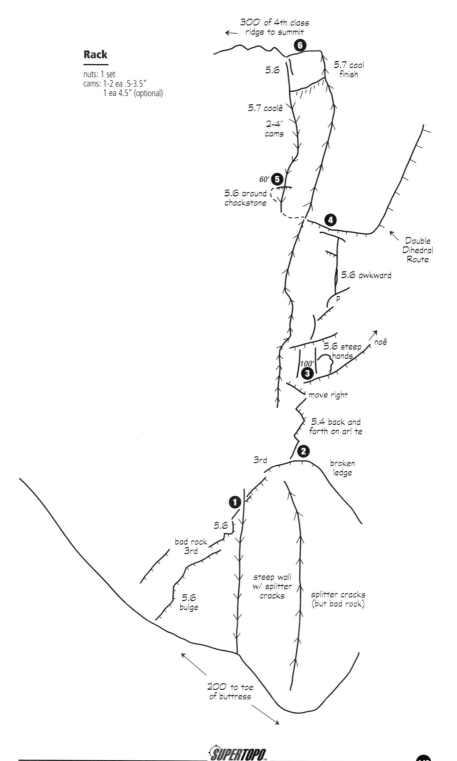

Rack

nuts: 1 set
cams: 1-2 ea .5-3.5"
         1 ea 4.5" (optional)

300' of 4th class
← ridge to summit

❻

5.6

5.7 cool
finish

5.7 coolê

2-4"
cams

60' ❺

5.6 around
chockstone

❹

Double
Dihedral
Route

5.6 awkward

p

noê

5.6 steep
hands

100'

❸

move right

5.4 back and
forth on ari te

❷

3rd

broken
ledge

❶

5.6

bad rock
3rd

steep wall
w/ splitter
cracks

splitter cracks
(but bad rock)

5.6
bulge

200' to toe
of buttress

Incredible Hulk

The Incredible Hulk (11,120') is known for three things: the best rock in the High Sierra, long routes, and incredibly sustained climbing. There are no easy routes on this face and, unlike most Sierra climbs, the Incredible Hulk remains sustained and challenging for a majority of the pitches (there are few pitches on any route easier than 5.8). The rock is clean and relatively unfractured and is more reminiscent of Yosemite climbing than the typical High Sierra peak. The climbs are challenging enough and just far enough from the road to eliminate crowds.

Approach

The trailhead for the Incredible Hulk is at Twin Lakes, 13 miles west of the town of Bridgeport. Take U.S. 395 to the north end of Bridgeport, turn west onto the Twin Lakes Road and drive to its end in the Mono Village at the west end of western lake. There is a $5 parking fee.

The approach takes most climbers 3-4 hours from Twin Lakes to the base of the climb (double approach times if you are carrying a heavy pack) and involves 2.5 miles on the main trail, 2.5 miles on climbers' trails and cross-country travel, and gains about 3,400 feet in elevation.

Finding the trailhead is difficult as you must navigate through the maze-like RV campground. (If getting a predawn start, scope out this section the day before.) Just try to follow the main road due west. After a few hundred yards you will turn right off the dirt road onto the Barney Lakes Trail that leads along Robinson Creek. Walk on this trail for about 45 minutes (2.5 miles) to a wilderness sign, a few hundred yards before Little Slide Canyon. It is legal to mountain bike all the way to the wilderness sign. This will save you some time on the way in and a lot of time on the way out.

From the sign, turn left and walk cross-country southwest, angling toward Robinson Creek. After 100 yards, look for an opportunity to cross the creek at a series of beaver dams. Many people get lost here. If you find yourself in a big marsh with tall grass, you should probably reverse your steps and find a crossing farther east. Flip flops or an extra pair of shoes and socks are strongly recommended. After the crossing, walk along the west shore of Robinson Creek for a few hundred feet before locating a climbers' trail that enters a prominent grove of pine trees on the east side of Little Slide Canyon. The trail ascends steep dirt switchbacks through these trees for the next few hundred yards. Do not walk up the middle of Little Slide Canyon or you will be bushwhacking forever.

The switchbacks eventually flatten and, after another few hundred yards, the trail ends in talus. From here, the approach is hard to follow. Stay on the left (east) side of the canyon and follow the edge of the talus until you are forced into it. Continue up to a cliff band. Here you have two options: Either avoid the cliff band by hiking up and left around it up horrible steep scree, or look for a 3rd class scramble up the cliff band.

To avoid the way, hike (3rd class) up the cliff band. For the next 0.25 mile, it is hard to give good directions so you will have to rely mostly on your intuition. The general idea is to go up the gully and, when possible, over right to the next gully. The correct gully will take you on the right (east) of a granite formation and almost to Maltby Lake. When below the Incredible Hulk, it will be obvious how to make the final approach up the talus.

The scree way is less direct, involves lots of "two steps forward, one step back" terrain, but you are less likely to get lost. Heading up the cliff band is more direct, but because you stay in the canyon it is difficult to see where you are. Both ways are difficult to describe—use your routefinding skills. You basically follow the canyon up until beneath the Incredible Hulk and then hike up talus to the base.

Incredible Hulk. (Chris McNamara)

Sun Spot Dihedral

Positive Vibrations

Red Dihedral

Falling Dihedral Variation

Descent

The descent takes about 45 minutes to get from the summit to the base of the route and another 2-3 hours to get back to Twin Lakes. Only one 50m or 60m rope is required for the one rappel on the descent. From the summit, downclimb the steep 3rd class on the south ridge (opposite direction of the climbing route) for about 300 feet to a rappel anchor (bolts and slings). It helps to locate the rappel anchors when you are about 40 feet below the summit. Make an 80-foot rappel to the notch between two gullies: one leads to the north (toward Twin Lakes) one leads to the south (away from Twin Lakes). Take the south gully (the north gully is usually filled with ice and really dangerous). Downclimb 3rd class for a few hundred yards. When the gully opens up, stay left (staying right sends you over a steep cliff). Eventually gain the main talus and scree gully that wraps around to the base of the climbs. Reverse the approach.

If you need motivation for the descent, think of the burgers and fries that await at the trailhead grill (open until 9 p.m.).

Little Slide Canyon

beaver dams

The view from where you will leave the main trail. An aspen grove is just out of view to the right.

Backcountry Camping

Some parties will want to bivy near the base of the route. There is excellent camping at certain points along the approach next to the river and there is a large flat area below Maltby Lake, just below the climb. You will need a wilderness permit—available by mail or in person at the Bridgeport Ranger Station. For more info visit: http://www.fs.fed.us/htnf/hoover.htm. At the same web address, you will also find information on the many different campgrounds that are located near the trailhead.

The two arrows show the crux of the approach. Either stay right in the gully or take the steep scree slope to the left.

Campground · restaurant
Mono Village
Twin Lakes
7100'
Robinson Creek
Robinson Creek Trail
WL 10,427
7111'

wilderness sign
beaver dams
steep switchbacks in pines

Horsetail Falls

Little Slide Canyon

Slide Canyon

talus

WILDERNESS
BOUNDARY

Horse Creek

Horse Creek

HOOVE

10441'

Blacksmith

VF61-C
6-75

9578'

R 23 E
R 24 E

VF61-E
6-162

TIONAL   FOREST

Incredible Hulk
11280'

Little Slide Canyon

WILDERNESS
10139'

Glacier Lake
WL 10,025'?

Avalanche Lake
WL 9,?89'?

Horse

The Cleaver

WL 9,944'
Ice Lake

10691'

SAWTOOTH

MONO CO.
TUOLUMNE CO.

RIDGE

lake
(bivy spot)

PACK

N

Matterhorn Peak
12,279'

Burro Pass

MONO CO.
TUOLUMNE CO.

6-160

Peaks

Springs

park service trail — · — · — · —

climbers' trail — — — — —

cross-country travel · · · · · · · · ·

climbing route ————

distance between contour lines = 50 ft.

Sun Spot Dihedral 5.11b★★★★

Time to climb route:	**3-4 hours**
Approach time:	**3-4 hours**
Descent time:	**7-10 hours**
Sun exposure:	**sunset**
Height of route:	**1,500'**

This is harder than Positive Vibrations and of similar exceptional quality. If you thought Positive Vibrations was sustained then wait until you get on this! Pitches 3-6 rarely have a move easier than 5.10 and are steep, thin, and exposed. In addition, most of the pitches are 160 feet or longer, meaning you need to conserve gear and manage your pump. The route is named after the striking "Sun Spot," a 40' x 80' section of red rock halfway up the face. The route has mostly thin climbing: fingerlocks, stemming, and occasional hand jams. There are no fist, offwidth, or chimney moves on the route. No pitches are runout, but there are a few heads-up sections. You should be able to cruise The Rostrum before jumping on this route. The fact that a large corner system like this wasn't climbed until 1999 shows how many new routes are left in the High Sierra.

FA: Dave Nettle, Jimmy Haden, 9/99.

History

In the 1990s, hard-driving Tahoe climber Dave Nettle became the most active climber on Incredible Hulk. After climbing the established classics he began to glass the peak for new routes, and, left of Positive Vibrations, he focused on a prominent dihedral marked with a disc of red rock. He made two attempts in his favorite style: non-stop from car-to-car, or even house-to-house. So both times he started up what he'd dubbed Sun Spot Dihedral right after making the tough hike in. In each case he began with difficult, unclimbed cracks that met the top of the first pitch of Positive Vibrations. After 30 feet up that route, he branched left, and found hard going and marginal protection. On the second attempt he led a third pitch, up a beautiful straight-in crack until it petered out, and he drilled a protection bolt that allowed him to reach a belay stance. From there, he looked up at more terrain that looked both alluring and intimidating. Overhangs loomed above, and beyond them the soaring, architecturally clean walls of the dihedral met at a joint that looked desperately thin. All in all, Nettle knew he'd started a spectacular line, but to climb it free might require a team with some pretty advanced horsepower.

In the summer of 1999, Nettle came back with a younger, super-talented Tahoe climber, Jimmy Haden. Haden insisted that they hike in and camp below the peak, to get a fresh morning start. With Nettle's previous experience and protection and belay bolts in place, they made good time up the first pitches. Next, Nettle found holds that let him lead through the overhangs with a few protection bolts. Then Haden started up the intimidating dihedral. To their surprise, he found that its thin seam periodically opened into digit-wide slots for fingers and gear. He made steady, exhilarating progress, stemming and bridging to make his way to the next fingerlock. After half a rope length, he stepped right to another corner, and worked this up to a flake. As he neared the end of his 60-meter rope, he pulled on the top of the flake and it peeled right off. Haden took a 30-foot plummet, but thankfully a good cam held the fall. The TV-sized flake

Sun Spot Dihedral		Pitch 1	2	3	4	5	6	7	8	9	10	11	12
Free difficulty	≥5.10	●	●	●	●	●	●		●	●			
	5.9							●			●		
	5.8											●	
	5.7												●
	5.6												
	≤5.5												

continued dropping and crashed away from Nettle, sending reports echoing around the canyon.

Haden had some bruised ribs, but he pulled up the lost 30 feet, and made a belay. Nettle decided to call this the Shooting Star Pitch. Another hundred feet of superb climbing took them right, to meet the splitter crack that forms the last pitch of Positive Vibrations. They finished with plenty of time to hike out that evening.

– Andy Selters

Strategy

The route is shaded almost all day, so it's best to climb in warmer temps. Luckily, it is reasonably sheltered from the wind. A 60m rope is mandatory.

There are two starts: the original start to the right, or up Positive Vibrations. Both are about the same difficulty, but the Positive Vibrations start is more direct.

Pitch 3 is probably the spookiest pitch. Be sure to use long slings on the initial roof traverse so the rope doesn't run over sharp edges. The last 30 feet to the belay are insecure and have bad pro. Either belay off the bolt and a 1" cam or from the stance to the left. Neither belay is that great.

Pitch 4 is stunning. Because the corner leans, the entire 170 feet feel slightly overhanging. The crux is low where you have to make committing technical stemming moves with RPs and tiny nuts for protection. From there the climbing is unrelenting 5.10 to the anchor. Conserve cams so you have enough for the end of the pitch and the anchor.

Chris McNamara

Todd Offenbacher enjoys a rare rest on the Sun Spot Dihedral.

Pitch 5 starts with the technical crux of the route: powerful face moves on an overhanging wall. The first clip is hard and committing (you might be able to get RPs before it.) One more incredible sustained pitch leads to the North Ridge finish. These last five or so pitches are pretty lame. The rock is mostly loose and easy, but you have to make the occasional 5.9 and 5.10 move.

Retreat

Retreat by rapping the route and leaving gear behind. With two ropes you will be able to leave less gear.

Positive Vibrations

5.11a★★★★★

Time to climb route:	**3-4 hours**
Approach time:	**3-4 hours**
Descent time:	**8-12 hours**
Sun exposure:	**noon to sunset**
Height of route:	**1,500'**

Positive Vibrations is possibly the best rock climb in the High Sierra. It takes a proud line up a ridiculously exposed prow in the center of the face. The rock quality is exceptional and the climbing is unrelenting with the first eight pitches rated 5.10 or harder. The climb has an even balance of finger and hand cracks with no wide sections. The route feels about as hard as Yosemite's Rostrum but is longer and more committing.

FA: Bob Harrington, Alan Bartlett, 7/81.
FFA: Dale Bard, Tom Lyde, 7/86.

History

By the late 1970s, this whisper spread around a core circle of Tuolumne climbers: an obscure 11,000-foot peak dubbed Incredible Hulk held some of the best high country granite around. Mike Farrell's knowledge of it led Dale Bard and Bob Harrington into becoming two of the primary Hulk enthusiasts, and after they each had climbed a couple of routes on it, they teamed up with a plan to head for the impressive shield left of Red Dihedral (AKA Ygdrasil), the 1975 Farrell/Bard/Locke route. In 1977, Harrington and Bard began in the ledgy ramps below Ygdrasil's "red dihedral," and angled left up easy ground and three roped pitches to a big ledge at the base of the shield. Then they veered right to work up marginal cracks on the right side of the shield. After an awful bivouac, they finished what they agreed was a forgettable and scary route, which Bard called Millenium Falcon.

A couple of years later, Harrington returned with Rick Wheeler and Paul Brown with the idea to work straight up from that big ledge, aiming for cracks on the left side of the shield. They expected to resort to a fair bit of aid, and so brought bivouac gear to go for it after a night on that ledge. They fixed two sustained and excellent pitches above the ledge and settled in for the night, but a storm came in. In the morning's gale they retreated, but when they pulled the rope, the wind whipped it around a corner and into a crack, and they struggled through a minor epic to retrieve it and get down.

Harrington came back again in 1981, this time with Alan Bartlett. As they hiked in, an afternoon thunderstorm bombed the area with hail and lightning, and they knew that the following day could likely bring the same. Despite the consequences of being caught high in an electrical storm, they decided to race the weather. Harrington's previous experience helped them work quickly up to the ledge and onto the shield, where they free climbed some sections where Harrington had aided before, yet they also had to use aid on a few moves that had previously gone free. The morning was still young, but a few clouds were already forming. The race was looking serious, but the cracks in the upper shield turned out to be excellent. They stemmed and pulled on jam after jam and occasional gear to make time, and by about 11 a.m. they were on the summit. They called their new route

Positive Vibrations	Pitch	1	2	3	4	5	6	7	8	9	10	11	12	13
Free difficulty	≥5.10	●	●	●	●	●	●	●	●					
	5.9													
	5.8									●	●	●	●	
	5.7													●
	5.6													
	≤5.5													

Positive Vibrations, recalling a Bob Marley song and the way the route and their optimistic style had come together so very nicely. Few subsequent teams have made such good time.

Dale Bard came back in 1986 with Tom Lyde, a co-worker at Patagonia. Psyched with the expectation that he had a good chance of climbing the route free, Bard led every pitch. With some of the best crack technique in the world, he freed the route, including the upper shield at 5.11a, and Lyde followed free too.

In 1999 Tom Lyde died in a rappelling accident, and Bard proposed that the free climb be named Lyde's Ride, but it seems unlikely that this name will catch on. Today the favorite line starts way left, with four hard pitches that were originally climbed with some aid by Rick Wheeler and Dave Bircheff, when they completed the Macedonian Route in about 1975.

– Andy Selters

Strategy

Crowds are hit or miss. Because this route is so good, it sometimes has a few parties. However, because the climb is pretty hard, you will usually have it to yourself. Bring a 60m rope.

The climb is long and demanding, therefore most climbers should start by 8 a.m. or earlier. The first four pitches are shady and sometimes bitterly cold until around 2 p.m., but are thankfully sheltered from the wind. The upper four pitches come into the sun around noon and are extremely exposed to the wind. When high winds are forecasted, pick another route. If you hit Pitch 4 and the winds are intense, one option is to climb the ramps and crack system up and right (some 5.10 but mostly easier) and join up with Red Dihedral somewhere between Pitches 6 and 8.

The first few pitches warm you up for the difficulties above. The third pitch has a devious but short boulder problem crux. Pitch 6 is the endurance crux featuring unrelenting 5.10 moves to a pumpy boulder problem crux up top. Belaying at the bolt before the crux makes this pitch easier but not as cool. The next few pitches are long, pumpy, and will feel like stiff 5.10 if you, like most mortals, are tired by now. And the route keeps going! After Pitch 8, either keep to the ridge for the best rock or drop onto the north side for easier climbing but looser rock. Finish on Red Dihedral.

Retreat

You can retreat from Pitch 3 with one 60m rope if you leave slings and maybe some gear at the first belay. It's easy to retreat from Pitch 5 with two ropes. Above Pitch 5, you will need to leave gear whether you have a 50m or 60m rope.

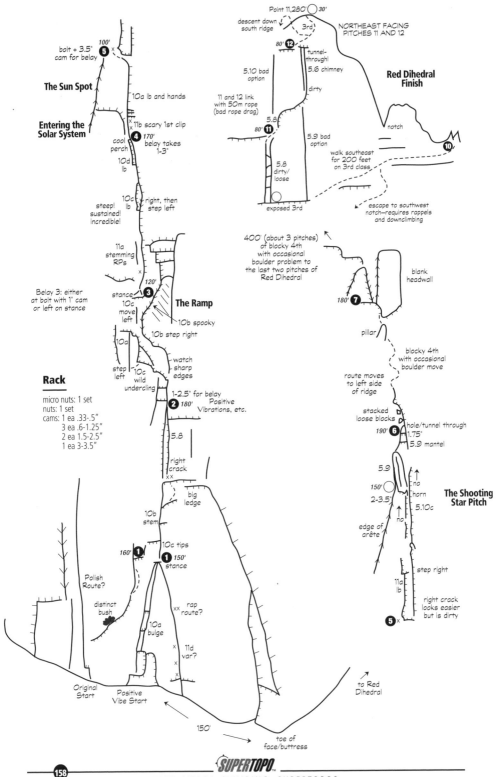

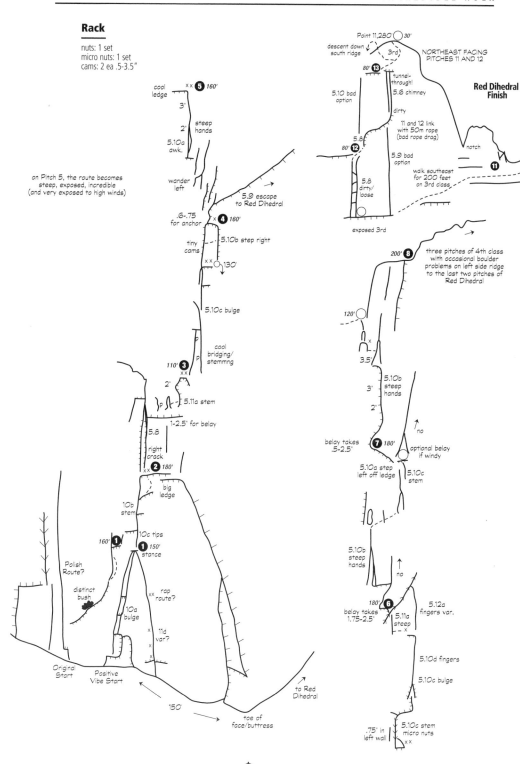

Rack

nuts: 1 set
micro nuts: 1 set
cams: 2 ea .5-3.5"

cool ledge   xx **5** *160'*
3'
2'   steep hands
5.10a awk.

on Pitch 5, the route becomes
steep, exposed, incredible
(and very exposed to high winds)

wander left

5.9 escape
to Red Dihedral

.6-.75 for anchor   x **4** *160'*
5.10b step right
tiny cams

xx ○ *130'*

5.10c bulge

cool bridging/ stemming

110' **3**
xx
2'

5.11a stem
1-2.5" for belay

5.8
right crack
xx **2** *180'*

big ledge

10b stem

10c tips
160' **1**
1 *150'* stance

Polish Route?

distinct bush
xx   rap route?

10a bulge
x   11d var?
x

Original Start   Positive Vibe Start

150'   to Red Dihedral

toe of face/buttress

Point 11,280' ○ *30'*

descent down south ridge   3rd   NORTHEAST FACING
PITCHES 11 AND 12

80' **13**

5.10 bad option   tunnel-through!
5.6 chimney   **Red Dihedral Finish**

dirty

11 and 12 link
with 50m rope
(bad rope drag)   notch

5.8
80' **12**

5.9 bad option

walk southeast
for 200 feet
on 3rd class   **11**

5.8
dirty/ loose

exposed 3rd

200' **8**   three pitches of 4th class
with occasional boulder
problems on left side ridge
to the last two pitches of
Red Dihedral

120' ○
x
3.5'

5.10b steep hands
3'
2'
↑ no

belay takes
.5-2.5"   **7** *180'*   optional belay
if windy

5.10a step
left off ledge   5.10c stem

5.10b steep hands
↑ no

180' **6**
belay takes
1.75-2.5"   5.12a fingers var.
5.11a steep
x

5.10d fingers

5.10c bulge

.75" in left wall   5.10c stem micro nuts
xx

Red Dihedral 5.10b★★★★★

Time to climb route:	**6-10 hours**
Approach time:	**3-4 hours**
Descent time:	**3-4 hours**
Sun exposure:	**noon to sunset**
Height of route:	**1,200'**

Red Dihedral is the most moderate classic route on the Incredible Hulk but is still sustained and challenging (only one pitch is easier than 5.8). The rock is perfect, clean, golden granite and unlike most Sierra climbs, the route requires a fair amount of straight-in jamming technique (all the cruxes are on crack, not face). This is one of those few peaks that is much larger than it looks. From the base and approach, the upper pitches are not visible so when you get up on the climb it keeps going and going and going.

FA: Dale Bard, Mike Farrell, Bob Locke, 6/75.

History

Though the Incredible Hulk is a west-facing wall well-hidden from any road, it was the site of a fairly early Yosemite-esque wall climb in the High Sierra. In 1970 the trio of Greg Donaldson, Joe Kiskis, and Bob Grow spent a couple of days climbing through the center of the face. After completing the route at V, 5.8, A3 they made three rappels down the opposite side.

During the following years, the free-climbing revolution took hold in Yosemite. Among the revolutionaries, Dale Bard was the first to make a steady diet of desperate 5.11 cracks. In the spring of 1975, Bard took a ski tour that happened to run past "The Hulk," and right away he knew it had spectacular free-climbing potential. In June he organized two other Valley regulars to put aside their Tuolumne Meadows plans. They hiked into a campsite with an Italian motif to their banter, in honor of a group of Italian compatriots who had had a particularly tough season in Yosemite. Thus they knew themselves as "Dalessandro Bardini," "Roberto Lockoni" (Bob Locke) and "Enzo Farrelli" (Mike Farrell).

Packing in a rack of only hexes and stoppers, the three headed for a prominent red corner, the rightmost of two on the wall. They swung leads, calling out in mock Italian as wave clouds formed over the Sierra. As they continued above the crux corner, winds began to buffet them. At one stance Bard was knocked off, but Farrelli grabbed him by the gear sling before he could take a nasty fall. They completed the first technical route to tag the summit, and descended in time to hike out. Locke was a well-read literature major, and he suggested that they name the route for Ygdrasil, the ash tree of ancient Nordic mythology that symbolizes the blossoming forces of life surrounded by the waters of death.

Editors Note: In spite of the first ascensionists wishes, over time the route became known as Red Dihedral. Since every current climber and guidebook refers to the route as Red Dihedral, we also do to avoid confusion.

– Andy Selters

Red Dihedral	Pitch	1	2	3	4	5	6	7	8	9	10	11	12
Free difficulty	≥5.10				●			●					
	5.9	●	●		●	●		●	●				
	5.8	●			●							●	●
	5.7												
	5.6								●				
	≤5.5												

Strategy

Most climbers do the climb car-to-car in one HUGE day. Get a predawn start and move fast. Descending from the summit (specifically, finding the rappel) is difficult and dangerous in the dark. If you are not confident in your hiking and climbing speed, then camp below the climb. The route is moderately popular—you may see two other parties or you may see no one. A 60m rope is not mandatory but lets you do the route in as few as eight pitches.

The first half of the climb is sustained and follows major crack systems. The second half ascends more broken rock on easier terrain with the occasional 5.8 or 5.9 section. The line is distinct and easy to follow for the first four pitches. Pitch 2 is the only pitch on the climb that is difficult to protect.

Pitch 4, The Red Dihedral, is one of the more memorable pitches in the Sierra. Sustained hand jams lead to wild stemming moves through a bulge, followed by an airy traverse right on broken and steep 5.8. Some may want to bring extra cams in the 1-1.5" range. Save some bigger cams for the belay.

Above, the routefinding becomes more challenging so follow the topo closely and, when in doubt, climb straight up. There are many options for Pitches 7-10.

Once you reach the summit ridge (Belay 10) the rock quality deteriorates for the final pitch. It is crucial to walk over on 3rd class ledges to the obvious double cracks. At the top of the pitch, the wild tunnel through the chimney will be really hard with a pack. This is the only lame pitch on the climb, and you may need to break this into two pitches to avoid rope drag. Do not try to reach the summit by staying on the west face as the cracks become flared and bottoming.

Chris McNamara

Retreat

To retreat, rappel the route. It is easiest to retreat with two ropes, but it is possible to retreat with just one. Because there are no fixed belays on this climb, you will need to leave gear. High Sierra thunderstorms are common in the summer. Be sure to get the latest forecast before heading up on the route. The route can be exposed to very high winds making communication difficult.

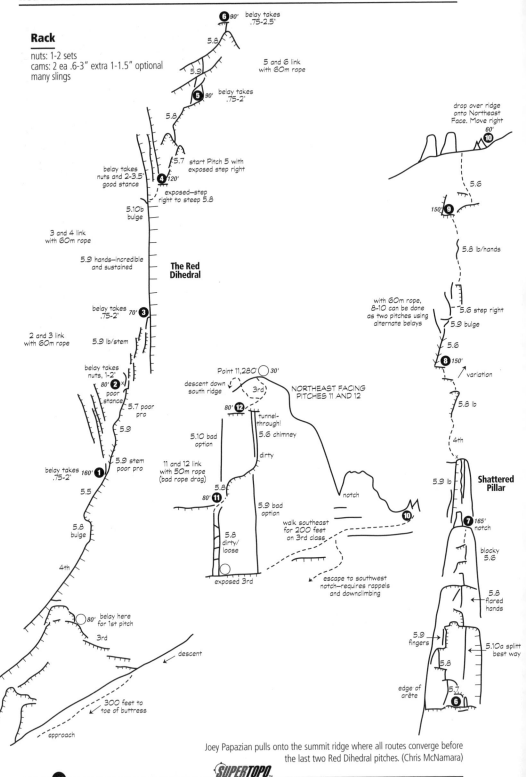

Rack
nuts: 1-2 sets
cams: 2 ea .6-3" extra 1-1.5" optional
many slings

6 90' belay takes .75-2.5"

5 and 6 link with 60m rope

5.8

5.9

5 90' belay takes .75-2'

5.8

drop over ridge onto Northeast Face. Move right
60'
10

5.7 start Pitch 5 with exposed step right

belay takes nuts and 2-3.5' good stance
4 120'

exposed–step right to steep 5.8

5.6

150' **9**

5.10b bulge

5.8 lb/hands

3 and 4 link with 60m rope

5.9 hands–incredible and sustained

The Red Dihedral

5.6 step right

5.9 bulge

with 60m rope, 8-10 can be done as two pitches using alternate belays

5.6

belay takes .75-2' 70' **3**

2 and 3 link with 60m rope

5.9 lb/stem

8 150'

variation

5.8 lb

belay takes nuts, 1-2'
80' **2** x
poor stance

5.7 poor pro

5.9

Point 11,280' ○ 30'

descent down south ridge 3rd

NORTHEAST FACING PITCHES 11 AND 12

80' **12**

tunnel-through!

5.6 chimney

4th
x

5.9 lb

Shattered Pillar

belay takes .75-2' 160' **1**

5.9 stem poor pro

5.10 bad option

5.8

dirty

11 and 12 link with 50m rope (bad rope drag)

80' **11**

5.9 bad option

notch

7 165' notch

5.5

walk southeast for 200 feet on 3rd class

blocky 5.6

5.8 bulge

5.8 dirty/ loose

10

5.8 flared hands

4th

exposed 3rd

escape to southwest notch–requires rappels and downclimbing

5.9 fingers

5.10a splitt best way

○ 80' belay here for 1st pitch

3rd

5.8

descent

300 feet to toe of buttress

5.7

edge of arête

6

approach

Joey Papazian pulls onto the summit ridge where all routes converge before the last two Red Dihedral pitches. (Chris McNamara)

Falling Dihedral 5.10a★★★

Time to climb route: **2 hours or less**

Approach time: **3-4 hours**

Descent time: **3-4 hours**

Sun exposure: **noon to sunset**

Height of route: **1,200'**

This is an easier and less classic start to Red Dihedral that bypasses crowds and cruxes. It's a good back up if Red Dihedral is too crowded or you are running short on time. The rock is not the Hulk's finest but is well protected at the 5.6-5.8 moves. Most of this variation is 4th class with only a few moves of 5.6-5.8 before joining Red Dihedral.

A Story

I call this the Falling Dihedral Variation because I think the initial pitches are on the Falling Leaf route. In the summer of 2003 I started up Positive Vibrations with Todd Offenbacher but a continuous 40+ mph wind beat us back at Pitch 5. Desperate to climb something that day but without enough time to use a rope, I waited until the wind died a few hours before sunset and started soloing Red Dihedral. My solo was short lived—the first crux spooked me and I backed off.

Now I was truly desperate to climb something before the day was over. I stepped away from the wall in the vain hope I could find more courage or an easier route. I found what appeared to be the latter a few hundred feet right of Red Dihedral. An hour before sunset, I started climbing with the strategy that there was so little daylight that I didn't have time to be scared. Fortunately, the route pieced itself together as I moved untethered over 1,000+ feet of granite cast in soft orange evening light. I stood on the summit right at sunset

and immediately began running down the descent. I paused only once to send a large round boulder on the longest trundle of my life: This boulder went from the top of the final gully to within a few hundred yards of camp. One thousand plus feet of great granite climbing and a big trundle—it doesn't get any better than that.

– Chris McNamara

Strategy

Because I soloed this route, I didn't have time or a rope to measure exact belay locations. Here is the basic route description: Walk a few hundred feet up and right of the Red Dihedral route. The route starts just left and a few hundred feet below a big left-facing red dihedral (don't confuse this with the red dihedral on the Red Dihedral route). Next, follow the line of least resistance up and left of a slabby bowl for a few hundred feet. This section is a grainy and not particularly classic 4th and easy 5th class ramp/corner. Eventually, a short 5.8 crack gets you through to a big easy traverse left to the Red Dihedral route. If you continue up right of the Red Dihedral, you may or may not be on the original 5.9 Falling Leaf route.

Rack

nuts: 1 set
cams: 2 ea .5-2.5"
      1 ea 3.5"

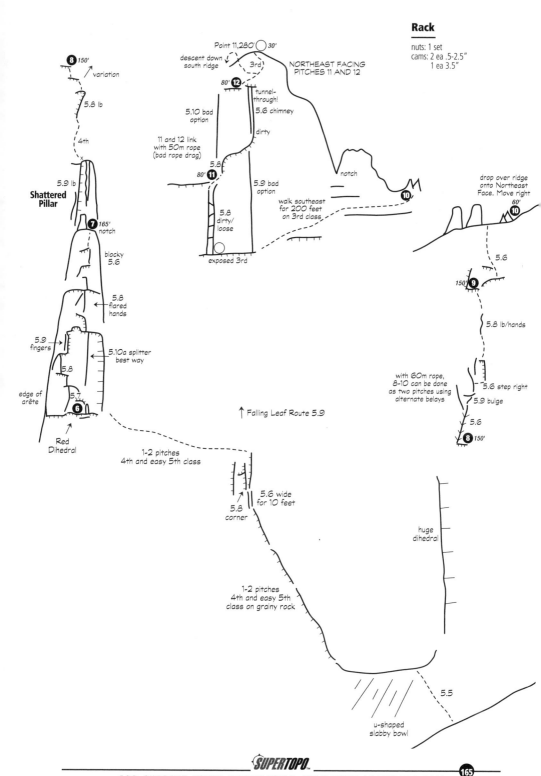

8 150'
→ variation
5.8 lb
4th

**Shattered
Pillar**

5.9 lb

7 165'
notch

blocky
5.6

5.8
flared
hands

5.9
fingers

5.10a splitter
best way

5.8

edge of
arête

5.7

6

↑
Red
Dihedral

1-2 pitches
4th and easy 5th class

Point 11,280' ◯ 30'
descent down
south ridge   3rd

80' **12**
tunnel-
through!

5.10 bad
option   5.6 chimney

11 and 12 link
with 50m rope   dirty
(bad rope drag)

80' **11**   5.8

5.8
dirty/
loose   5.9 bad
option

walk southeast
for 200 feet
on 3rd class

exposed 3rd

NORTHEAST FACING
PITCHES 11 AND 12

notch

10

↑ Falling Leaf Route 5.9

5.6 wide
for 10 feet

5.8
corner

1-2 pitches
4th and easy 5th
class on grainy rock

drop over ridge
onto Northeast
Face. Move right
60'
10

5.6

150' **9**

5.8 lb/hands

5.6 step right

with 60m rope,
8-10 can be done
as two pitches using
alternate belays   5.9 bulge

5.6

8 150'

huge
dihedral

5.5

u-shaped
slabby bowl

We need YOUR feedback

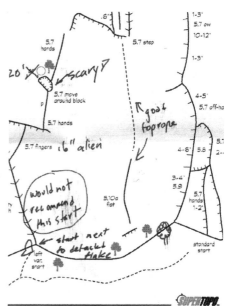

I love getting feedback on SuperTopos. The reason we make SuperTopos is so that you and other climbers can have an incredible experience on the rock. If there is any way I can make this experience better I want to know.

Every time you climb a route you will come away with a unique familiarity about each pitch. I want to hear what you thought of the climb and what you think can be improved on our topos. This information will help us make better topos and enhance other people's climbing experience.

Mail us your topo corrections and help make SuperTopos even better.

Subject: Some feedback on the SuperTopos
From: run@itout.com
To: chris@supertopo.com

The topos ruled. here is some feedback

Jam Crack ...
* Although the topo is very clear, you might want to add the words "15' left" after "....either belay 15' left at the bolted anchor or continue ....". The reason I say that is the first time I led the climb I just kept climbing up the very thin, maybe .10d section between the top of the 5.7 crack section and the bolts. It looked really hard so I down climbed and realized I was supposed to be further left.

After Six ...
* 1st Pitch ... You might (or not) want to repeat a comment I've heard several times that the 1st pitch is the "hardest 5.6 in the valley". It's awkward after the dead tree and on the polished section in the middle of the pitch ... gravity wants to pull you out of the crack to the right. It's OK after starting the traverse to the right.
* I've always belay at the ledge in the Manzanita bushes just to the left of where the 5.6 variation 2nd pitch goes up. It's solid using the bushes

---

You will greatly help us if after your climb you do one of two things:

• Visit the web site's Climber Beta section (www.supertopo.com/route_beta) and tell SuperTopo users about the climb. What were the conditions like? Is there any extra beta? What did you think of the route?

• If you have any suggestions, please email me at chris@supertopo.com or send snail mail to 2 Bradford Way, Mill Valley, CA 94941. Let me know if we got a pitch length wrong, if you disagreed with a rating, or if you think the topo could be better in any way.

Thank you for helping us improve SuperTopo,

Chris McNamara
Founder and CEO
SuperTopo

Brad Goya moves up the fifth pitch where the arête narrows and the exposure kicks in. (Chris McNamara)

Climbs by Rating

☐ Mt. Russell, East Ridge 3rd class★★★★ (62)
☐ Mt. Whitney, Mountaineer's Route 3rd class★★ (50)
☐ Laurel Mountain, Northeast Gully 5.2★★★ (106)
☐ Bear Creek Spire, Northeast Ridge 5.5★★★★ (99)
☐ Tenaya Peak, Northwest Buttress 5.5★★★★ (129)
☐ Cathedral Peak, Southeast Buttress 5.6★★★★★ (114)
☐ Mt. Conness, North Ridge 5.6★★★★ (135)
☐ Mt. Conness, West Ridge 5.6★★★★★ (140)
☐ Matterhorn Peak, North Arête 5.7★★★ (148)
☐ Matthes Crest, Traverse from South to North 5.7★★★★★ (124)
☐ Mt. Whitney, East Face 5.7★★★★★ (40)
☐ Mt. Whitney, East Buttress 5.7★★★★★ (46)
☐ Temple Crag, Venusian Blind 5.7★★★★★ (76)
☐ Bear Creek Spire, North Arête 5.8★★★★ (96)
☐ Charlotte Dome, South Face 5.8★★★★★ (68)
☐ Temple Crag, Moon Goddess Arête 5.8★★★★ (78)
☐ Eichorn's Pinnacle, West Pillar 5.9★★★ (119)
☐ Mt. Goode, North Buttress 5.9★★★ (89)
☐ Mt. Russell, Fishhook Arête 5.9★★★★★ (59)
☐ Incredible Hulk, Falling Dihedral 5.10a★★★ (164)
☐ Temple Crag, Sun Ribbon Arête 5.10a★★★★★ (82)
☐ Incredible Hulk, Red Dihedral 5.10b★★★★★ (160)
☐ Third Pillar of Dana, Regular Route 5.10b★★★★★ (110)
☐ Keeler Needle, Harding Route 5.10c★★★ (52)
☐ Mt. Conness, Southwest Face 5.10c★★★★ (143)
☐ Incredible Hulk, Positive Vibrations 5.11a★★★★★ (156)
☐ Incredible Hulk, Sun Spot Dihedral 5.11b★★★★ (154)

Climbs by Name

Bear Creek Spire, Northeast Ridge 5.5★★★★ (99)
Bear Creek Spire, North Arête 5.8★★★★ (96)
Cathedral Peak, Southeast Buttress 5.6★★★★★ (114)
Charlotte Dome, South Face 5.8★★★★★ (68)
Eichorn's Pinnacle, West Pillar 5.9★★★ (119)
Incredible Hulk, Falling Dihedral 5.10a★★★ (164)
Incredible Hulk, Positive Vibrations 5.11a★★★★★ (156)
Incredible Hulk, Red Dihedral 5.10b★★★★ (160)
Incredible Hulk, Sun Spot Dihedral 5.11b★★★★ (154)
Keeler Needle, Harding Route 5.10c★★★ (52)
Laurel Mountain, Northeast Gully 5.2★★★ (106)
Matterhorn Peak, North Arête 5.7★★★ (148)
Matthes Crest, Traverse from South to North 5.7★★★★★ (124)
Mt. Conness, North Ridge 5.6★★★★ (135)
Mt. Conness, Southwest Face 5.10c★★★★ (143)
Mt. Conness, West Ridge 5.6★★★★★ (140)
Mt. Goode, North Buttress 5.9★★★ (89)
Mt. Russell, East Ridge 3rd class★★★★ (62)
Mt. Russell, Fishhook Arête 5.9★★★★★ (59)
Mt. Whitney, East Buttress 5.7★★★★★ (46)
Mt. Whitney, East Face 5.7★★★★★ (40)
Mt. Whitney, Mountaineer's Route 3rd class★★ (50)
Temple Crag, Moon Goddess Arête 5.8★★★★ (78)
Temple Crag, Sun Ribbon Arête 5.10a★★★★★ (82)
Temple Crag, Venusian Blind 5.7★★★★★ (76)
Tenaya Peak, Northwest Buttress 5.5★★★★ (129)
Third Pillar of Dana, Regular Route 5.10b★★★★★ (110)

MORE FROM SUPERTOPO

DESERT ADVENTURE CLASSICS
RED ROCKS CLIMBING (Print Book)
List Price: $24.95 Available at www.supertopo.com

Our *Red Rocks Climbing* guidebook provides SuperTopos for the best Red Rocks climbs—most in the 5.4 to 5.11 range. While the guidebook focuses on the most classic multi-pitch routes such as Crimson Chrysalis and Epinephrine, cragging routes are also included. Most of the climbs are on the highest quality sandstone Red Rocks has to offer and are well-protected with bolts or natural gear. This guide is perfect for climbers making their first trip to Red Rocks or returning climbers who want to tick off all the classics.

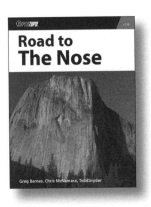

EVER WANTED TO CLIMB A BIG WALL?
ROAD TO THE NOSE (eBook)
List Price: $14.95 Available at www.supertopo.com

Many climbers consider The Nose of El Capitan the crowning achievement of a climbing career. In the *Road to The Nose*, big wall master Chris McNamara takes you through 14 climbs of increasing difficulty to help you build skills, speed, endurance, and comfort with big wall climbing. This guide includes special tips and beta specific to The Nose as well as more general information on getting ready for your first big wall.

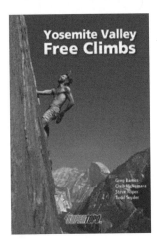

THE BEST TOPOS FOR YOSEMITE'S BEST CLIMBS
YOSEMITE VALLEY FREE CLIMBS (Print Book)
List Price: $29.95 Available at www.supertopo.com

This guidebook includes over 230 of the best routes in Yosemite Valley, from 16-pitch trad climbs to one-pitch sport routes. While many hard Yosemite testpieces are included, this book focuses on topropes, crags, and multi-pitch climbs in the 5.4-5.9 range. We also include formerly obscure climbs to provide more options for avoiding crowds. As in all SuperTopo books, the authors personally climbed and documented each route with meticulous care to create the most detailed and accurate topos ever published.

MORE FROM SUPERTOPO

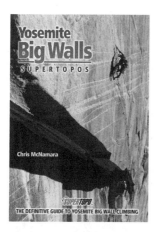

UNPRECEDENTED BIG WALL BETA
YOSEMITE BIG WALLS (Print Book)
List Price: $29.95 Available at www.supertopo.com

Written by Chris McNamara who personally climbed and painstakingly documented every route, this book includes essential route details such as climbing strategy, retreat information, descent topos, pitch lengths, and gear recommendations for each pitch. Yosemite Big Walls covers the 41 best big wall routes on El Capitan, Half Dome, Washington Column, and Leaning Tower.

OUTSTANDING PEAKS AND DOMES IN THE HIGH SIERRA
TUOLUMNE FREE CLIMBS (Print Book)
List Price: $24.95 Available at www.supertopo.com

Tuolumne Free Climbs includes over 110 of the best routes in Tuolumne Meadows from 14-pitch trad climbs to one-pitch sport routes. This book focuses on topropes, crags, and multi-pitch climbs in the 5.4-5.9 range. It includes formerly obscure climbs to provide more options for avoiding crowds. As in all SuperTopo books, the authors personally climbed and documented each climb with meticulous care to create the most detailed and accurate topos ever published.

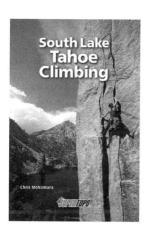

EXQUISITE YEAR-ROUND CLIMBING
SOUTH LAKE TAHOE CLIMBING (Print Book)
List Price: $24.95 Available at www.supertopo.com

South Lake Tahoe offers exquisite year-round climbing for every ability and taste. Trad climbers can jam smooth Yosemite-like cracks at Sugarloaf or Eagle Lake, pull on steep knobs at Phantom Spires, lead their first multi-pitch route at Lover's Leap. Sport climbers can clip bolts at Luther Rock, Luther Spires, and Mayhem Cove. This book focuses on some of the highest quality granite in the Sierra.

The Final Pitch

Chris McNamara

Thanks for buying this SuperTopo guidebook. We hope you enjoy it and the climbing adventure it may help you experience.

Your purchase means a lot to us. We here at SuperTopo are climbers who have set out to create a small business dedicated to giving you, and climbers like you, immediate access to the kind of detailed information you can normally only get by talking with a local expert. It takes a lot of work to create each SuperTopo and we're committed to making sure it's done right.

We're on a mission to develop SuperTopos for the best routes in the best climbing areas in North America. We hold ourselves strictly accountable to a high standard, namely that each of our SuperTopos offers the very finest quality route information obtainable anywhere on each and every route we cover.

If you found this SuperTopo guidebook useful, we'd like to ask you to tell your friends about SuperTopo. We're about as "grassroots" an organization as you can imagine, and are entirely dependent on word-of-mouth referrals to keep producing quality SuperTopos.

On behalf of myself and the rest of the crew here at SuperTopo, I want to thank you for your support. Keep climbing and please tell a friend about SuperTopo!

Thanks again,

Chris McNamara
Founder and CEO
SuperTopo

Chris McNamara

Climbing Magazine once computed that three percent of Chris McNamara's life on earth has been spent on the face of El Capitan—an accomplishment that has left friends and family pondering Chris' sanity. He's climbed El Capitan over 50 times and holds nine big wall speed climbing records. In 1998 Chris did the first Girdle Traverse of El Capitan, an epic 75-pitch route that begs the question, "Why?" *Outside Magazine* has called Chris one of "the world's finest aid climbers." He's the winner of the 1999 Bates Award from the American Alpine Club and founder of the American Safe Climbing Association, a nonprofit group that has replaced over 3,000 dangerous anchor bolts. He also serves on the board of directors of the Access Fund.

Dan Patitucci preparing to scree surf down the Mountaineer's Route. (PatitucciPhoto)